Painful
Blessing

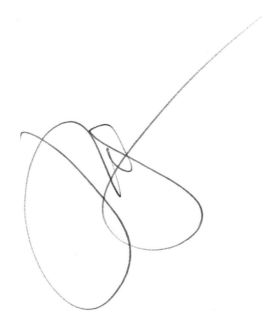

Painful Blessing

A Story of Loss, Recovery, Hope, and the Faith That Carries Us *When Our Own Strength Is Insufficient*

Jill Krantz Viggiano

Painful Blessing

The trade paperback edition of this book is for sale at

- Amazon.com
- BarnesandNoble.com
- BooksaMillion.com
- ChristianBook.com
- CreateSpace.com
- other online book retailers

Customized editions of this book are available in quantities of 99 or more. Please contact Jill@mybrainllc.com.

While you're online, please visit www.MyBrainllc.com, where you can see media coverage of this amazing story, scan a list of the 100+ events where Gordon and Jill have spoken so far, read Gordon's often humorous and always true-to-life posts, and invite them to speak at one of your upcoming events.

You're welcome to share your own story and request prayer by writing to Gordon@mybrainllc.com.

To Gordon,
the hardest working and
most optimistic man I ever met.

To Rachel,
Daddy's Little Girl, strong and wise.

To Tom,
a young man with depth and purpose.

Contents

Why I Wrote This Book

Acquired Brain Injury can be caused by a stroke and is devastating, scary, and highly individual. I wrote this book because I am sure we are not the only people to face the fear and uncertainty that greet us every day due to this life-changing event. I am also sure that the crazy, disturbing things my husband said and did in his recovery are not unique to him. It was terrifying for me to have no warning or frame of reference for what was coming our way.

I wrote this book because there has been no miraculous event that allowed us to circumvent the hard work—and indomitable team work—that recovery requires. This is not an "I did it and you can too" story. This is a personal story of recovery from the trenches. I wrote this book so that others who might have similar experiences won't feel so alone. Never forget: recovery is a team sport.

I wrote this book because our story brings hope to many who are struggling. Our story happens to be about stroke, but trouble comes for all of us—no one is immune. As the Bible says, the foundation on which your life is built will determine how you weather the storm. We encourage people to examine the foundations and priorities of their own lives now, before the day of crisis hits.

I wrote this book to show that even after a life-changing event, there is still much hope, love, and happiness to be had. It may not look the same as it did before the event, but that's okay. When our lives are broken, we have the opportunity to pick up the pieces we want to keep and assemble them in new ways. We may even pick up new pieces and put together a life we couldn't have imagined before the event. Not that it is easy—it isn't—but sometimes it is the only choice we have.

After you read this book, would you please consider writing a brief note to Gordon at <u>Gordon@MyBrainllc.com</u> or to me at <u>Jill@MyBrainllc.com</u>? That would mean the world to us.

We hope to hear from you soon.

Sunday, March 30, 2008

Dear Friends of the Viggiano Family,

I am writing on behalf of Gordon and Jill to let you know that Gordon had a stroke early Friday morning. He has had surgery to open the artery, and is recovering better than anyone had anticipated–something being widely credited to his excellent health, but as we friends of Gordon all know, his remarkable loving spirit must be playing a major role.

He has very limited movement in his right arm and hand, and yet even as of today that was changing and improving moment by moment. He has not regained full speech, but today began to form some words. It is still early and not everything is known, and he is not out of the woods. But given that it was a major event, everything about this early stage of his recovery is extraordinarily remarkable— as is Gordon.

Jill and the kids are showering Gordon with love. It has been extremely hard for them, but they are holding tight. We all know that Jill is amazing; her grace and clarity at this time have been nothing short of absolutely inspirational. Your love and support for all four of them certainly will be felt and much appreciated.

This is going to be a tough journey.

Liana Winett

1

Tough Journey, Indeed

It was 2008 and Gordon and I had a life plan that was
finally coming together. In 2001, we moved to Oregon with
our kids, Rachel and Tommy, anxious to leave the hectic,
crowded life in California. Gordon began a sales consulting
practice and I was blessed to now be a full-time mom. We
had some very lean years as we got the business going but we
stuck to the plan and our consulting practice was thriving.

We were finally earning enough to pay ourselves back the
money we spent during Gordon's start-up years. We were
saving for retirement and college. We went to church on
Sundays and we donated to our favorite charities. Things
seemed to be going our way and we appreciated it.

March 27th 2008 was a particularly wonderful day. It was
Spring Break. Rachel, a 9th grader, and Tommy, a 7th
grader, were enjoying the lazy, sleep-in days of no school. I
was just as happy to not set the alarm clock. Gordon had
turned 51 the day before and had just closed a big deal,
bringing him over his revenue goal for the quarter. He played
squash with his buddies that evening, and when he came
home, we talked excitedly about a short vacation that was
coming up.

It was a beautiful moment in time. I didn't think life could
get much better! We felt like we had the most important

elements to a happy life. We had close friends, we came from happy families, our house was filled with laughter, and we knew that God had blessed us with many gifts. We went to bed that night happy, healthy, and without the slightest inkling that everything we knew as normal, everything we had, everything we believed in, were about to be put to the test in a dramatic way.

It was three in the morning when Gordon woke me up and calmly asked if we could talk. Instantly, my mind began racing toward all the things my husband of 18 years might feel the need to say at three in the morning: I had an affair, I want to move, I'm not happy, I want to go to cowboy camp... Seriously, who wakes another person up at 3am just to talk?

Gordon told me that he couldn't see out of his left eye. He had gotten up to go to the bathroom and noticed something was odd. Oozy globs were passing in front of his vision, like a dark lava lamp. In true low-key Gordon fashion, he came back to bed, sweetly asked me if I wanted to talk, and told me the disturbing news.

I shot out of bed like the mattress was on fire.

I called our eye doctor and he said we should go to the ER "just in case," which we did immediately. We let the kids sleep—no reason to disturb them. I put a note on Rachel's bedroom door, telling her where we were going, just in case she woke up.

Other than the problem with Gordon's left eye, he seemed completely fine. It had started to rain, so once we parked the car we even jogged into the hospital. Gordon and I chatted as he lay on the hospital bed and waited for results from the

6

numerous tests. He had no pain. We talked about how weird the "eye thing" was but how he seemed to be perfectly okay. We talked about how much this ER visit was going to cost, since we carried only major medical health insurance. I looked at my watch, hoping we could get home before the kids woke up so they wouldn't worry.

The tests revealed nothing wrong. The brain scan showed nothing abnormal. The ER doctor concluded that Gordon probably had a detached retina and that he would have to go see an ophthalmologist in the morning. That didn't seem so bad. We jogged through the rain back to the car. It was 6am.

2

Oh, If It Were Only That Easy

Once we got home, I took the note off Rachel's door and crawled back into bed. I closed my eyes, relieved that Gordon was okay and a little stressed that we likely had just burned through about $5 grand with that ER visit.

Gordon went again to the bathroom before coming back to bed. I tried to relax, assuming the worst was over, when I heard a thump. I figured it was nothing, just Gordon bumping the glass shower door with his elbow—nothing unusual. Then there was a second thump: a loud, resounding thud like someone dropped a sack of potatoes on the floor, like a body hit the floor. Then silence.

I threw off the covers and ran to the bathroom door. I knocked and called Gordon's name but there was no answer. I opened the door and there he was, collapsed in the corner. It was 6:30am.

Gordon was completely non-responsive. I shouted his name and tried to move him. His body was awkwardly wedged between the toilet, the shower, and the wall. I couldn't find out if he was breathing or if his heart was beating because of the way he was lying.

My shouting and door pounding woke Rachel and Tommy, who burst out of their rooms, sleepy, confused, and scared. I yelled for Rachel to get the phone and then tried to keep calm while calling 9-1-1. It was still dark outside and our house can be difficult to find, so I told Rachel to turn on all the lights and wait by the front door to wave the ambulance toward our driveway. Tommy was crying quietly, standing completely still.

The emergency service team arrived in minutes. It took three men to pull Gordon out of the bathroom and carry him onto the bed. I explained to them what happened earlier with his left eye and how we had just gotten back from the hospital where the ER doctor hadn't found anything wrong. Obviously, something was terribly wrong.

The paramedic kept calling Gordon's name and poking him with a pin. There was no response. Gordon lay motionless on the bed, eyes slightly open. I kept thinking he would suddenly open them all the way, look around, and ask what all the craziness was about, but that didn't happen. His eyes were slightly open but clearly he wasn't seeing anything.

The paramedic started asking me questions: did Gordon take any medications, legal or not? My answer was no—he was healthy as an ox and certainly not a recreational drug user.

The life-altering decisions were just beginning.

The lead paramedic had a look on his face that said, "This is very bad." His voice was low, metered, and calm. He asked me if we had a hospital preference. We had always been an incredibly healthy family and didn't have any real hospital experience. When I hesitated, the paramedic quietly said, "You want to go to OHSU."

Practical as always, my first thought was that OHSU (Oregon Health and Science University) had never been a part of our health insurance plan. Taking Gordon to an out-of-network hospital meant we would be charged out-of-network fees and there would be no limit on our out-of-pocket expenses. Financial ruin was inevitable with this decision. Then again, the paramedic was telling me that Gordon's last, best chance was at OHSU: unlimited financial vulnerability versus what may well mean my husband's life.

The critical moment flashed by in an instant. There was no time to debate alternatives or look up other hospitals connected to our health plan. My husband was lying on the bed, by all appearances dying. My children were still as statues, crying next to me. All the paramedics in the room were looking at me, waiting for my answer.

There was no choice, really. I nodded and asked for directions to the hospital. OHSU was where Gordon would receive the best care. So, that's where we went, even though that implied potential bankruptcy for our family and the loss of every dream that we had ever worked to build. As they loaded Gordon into the ambulance, the head paramedic thoughtfully suggested that we wait a few minutes before following in my car so my kids wouldn't see the lights flashing or hear the siren if they had to use it.

It was a cold March and lightly snowing as we made our way up the hill to the hospital. It was spring break, so there were fewer cars on the road than usual. I had never been to the OHSU complex before, so it took us a while to find our way through the maze of buildings and winding roads. I have no recollection of parking or walking into the emergency room or asking where my husband was. I remember standing in the hall, beyond the secured double doors, and seeing the same paramedics walking toward me. They were leaving, their work was done. The head paramedic still had that grave look on his face when he wished me luck. I am not sure if I said anything.

We were shown to a very small room with a couple of chairs and a table in it. It looked like it may have been a closet at some time, but now it was where we waited. A social worker came in to talk to Rachel and Tommy while I was asked to follow a woman to a different room. There was Gordon, lying motionless, surrounded by doctors. Bright lights were shining on him.

One doctor told me Gordon was having a stroke and they were discussing how to proceed. I think they mentioned a couple of options and I think I responded, but more than anything, I remember looking at Gordon and expecting him to wake up. He looked like he was only sleeping. His eyes were completely shut now. *Open your eyes. Look at me. Tell me you are going to be fine.* But Gordon didn't move.

By the time I arrived, the doctors had already cut off most of Gordon's clothes. They asked if it would be all right if they shaved some of Gordon's body hair. Gordon is Italian. If there is one thing the Italians in Gordon's family excel at, it is growing body hair. Holding back tears, I made a joke about how he had plenty and wouldn't miss a few patches. I looked at Gordon's face, fully expecting to see a little smile, but there was no smile.

They sent me back to the waiting room/closet while they decided what to do. The social worker had taken Rachel to get something to eat. Tommy, practically motionless, waited for me.

The doctor's diagnosis was that both of Gordon's carotid arteries had dissected. Think of a plastic straw that has bent and has cracked and you will have a general idea of what a dissected artery looks like. The damage in his left carotid had caused many clots to form, and they eventually flowed up into his brain, which blocked the flow of blood and starved the left half of his brain. Thankfully, the right carotid, though damaged, didn't throw any clots, so the right side of his brain was receiving the necessary blood flow.

What to do now? I had read about the "clot busting" drug, but that was never mentioned. The neurosurgeons decided to try a clot retrieval. They would maneuver a small coil up through Gordon's femoral artery in his groin, all the way to the brain, try to catch clots in the coil, and pull them back out. They didn't know how many they would be able to retrieve but they thought this was the best course of action. I signed the permission papers.

In the meantime, we were moved to a bigger waiting room with chairs, a television, and a box full of leftover pieces from old children's board games. Ironically, an advertisement was running on the television, warning of stroke risk factors and emphasizing, in big, bold letters, "Time is Brain." My husband had no risk factors, was in the middle of a stroke, and five hours had passed since he woke me up to tell me about his eye. What would five hours mean to Gordon's brain? The doctors were preparing for a clot retrieval, but time was still ticking by. How much longer will his brain have to wait for restored blood flow? How long is too long? Tick tock, tick tock.

Ever practical, I had grabbed Gordon's wallet and cell phone on my way out the door to the hospital. Ever ignorant, I still had no idea just how serious our situation was. My first thought in the waiting room was "Gordon has appointments this morning!" I scrolled through his calendar and called the people who were expecting him. I left messages saying that Gordon was experiencing a medical emergency and would not be able to make their meeting.

In my mind, Gordon was having a stroke, the doctors were going to fix him, and after a few weeks—a few months, tops—he would be back to work. I didn't want his clients to think he was just a no-show and perhaps not want to work with him when he was better. He was a respected professional and I didn't want his reputation damaged.

I had given my phone to Rachel and instructed her to start making calls to my family and to certain friends. She needed something to do and I couldn't bring myself to make the calls. Slowly, my amazing support system began appearing in the waiting room. Scott, Gordon's work associate, came with his family. Liana, my long-time friend who works in Public Health, brought her family and didn't leave my side. My brother Brent and his wife Susan made the snowy, three-hour mountain drive from Bend.

Doctors and administrators came and went. Each had something important to tell me. I understood almost nothing and now have no recollection of anything they said. I think I was just waiting for someone to say something encouraging, something that matched my crazy belief that this was serious but that Gordon would be fine in a few months. Liana tried to help me through all the conversations and asked the questions I didn't even know to ask.

The doctors were very clear that the outcome of the surgery was unknown. What does that mean? I discovered exactly what that phrase meant when the organ donation lady showed up.

Organ. Donation. A chill runs down my spine just thinking about it. A trim, blonde woman in a white lab coat walked briskly into the waiting room. In a style very similar to a tour guide's, she began to list possible outcomes from Gordon's situation. Her words came at me fast and matter-of-factly. Words like "non-functioning human being" and "vegetative state" dispassionately flowed from her lips. She told me to be ready to make the "hard decisions."

As I suddenly began to comprehend the magnitude of the situation, I realized my 14-year-old daughter was next to me, listening to the whole conversation. Out of the corner of my eye, I could see Liana desperately making the "Cut!" sign under her chin, trying to get the woman to stop talking long enough to get Rachel away from those words. Too late. As the trim, blonde woman in the white lab coat walked briskly out of the waiting room, Rachel looked at me with that trusting look that kids have for their parents, and asked me what I was going to do.

I've never been a believer in candy coating life's challenges. I spent my childhood on a farm in Iowa and I was not sheltered from the realities of life and death. I had seen animals give birth. I had seen sick animals die. I had accompanied my brothers on the gruesome chore of burying dead, feral animals shot by my father when they disturbed the cattle or killed our pets. Even as a child, I understood death and dying. My daughter had experienced the death of a goldfish, but that was about it. But now here she was, 14 years old, asking if her dad was going to live, die, or become unrecognizable from the man she goofed around with only the day before.

I asked her what she thought Dad would want me to do. My sweet, wise Rachel, Daddy's Little Girl, said, "If he is going to have to live in a bed, I don't think he wants to live that way." I agreed. We sat quietly together, waiting for the next round of doctors to come.

Hours later, a doctor came in to show me the scans of Gordon's arteries before and after the clot retrieval. They removed three large clots but had to leave the rest. *Seriously? You're going to leave clots in his head? Aren't clots doing the damage? Aren't clots the enemy here?* I had no idea what to do with that piece of information.

Small amounts of blood were now traveling to Gordon's left brain but the left carotid artery was badly damaged. Confidentially, the surgeon told our friend who is also a doctor at the hospital, that there was a good chance Gordon would lose the entire left side of his brain. Only time would tell if he would remain a functioning human being. Only time would tell if I would have to have a more specific conversation with the blonde woman in the white lab coat. Then again, there was no more for us to do at the hospital that night. We would have to come back the next day to see what we had to deal with.

Time to go home. Time to walk in the door and not have my husband with me. My mother, Brent, and Susan were already

16

in the kitchen, trying to create some sense of life in the house. It was dark outside. The message light on our answering machine blinked and blinked. My neighbor so sweetly brought over a casserole so we had something to eat. Oh, the kindness of people when disaster strikes! Yet I could eat only a few bites.

The unreality of what had happened and the reality of it all pounded in my brain and my mind kept vacillating between "This can't be happening" and "What Next?" We all moved mechanically, as if we had been smacked in the head and couldn't quite get our thoughts together.

I got down to the business part of What Next. I made phone calls to our closest friends—I didn't want them to hear about Gordon through the grapevine. I put together an email list so we could inform our friends and family what had happened. I pulled out my health insurance file to see if there was something I needed to do immediately. My mother and my brother pulled out their checkbooks and wrote checks, splitting part of the deductible between them so I wouldn't have to think about that. I love my practical family.

Bedtime. So awful. Rachel and Tommy retreated to their rooms, exhausted, emotionally wrung out, scared. As usual, I sat with them and answered their questions as best I could, and we said prayers together.

What do you pray for in this situation? Let Gordon survive? What if he survives but is in the vegetative state that the blonde woman in the white lab coat hinted at? Let Gordon die? I could never pray that prayer! Let him be a miracle who suddenly pops out of bed, totally fine? Get a hold of yourself! I prayed that the good Lord would love Gordon and hold him in His hands. We would just have to trust Him to do what was best.

I turned off all the lights and crawled into my cold bed. I was exhausted but I couldn't quite fall asleep. I heard a door open and footsteps coming into my room; it was my sweet Tommy. Quietly, he walked up beside me and put his hand on my shoulder.

I asked Tommy if he needed something. "No," he said. "You always tuck me in at night. I thought tonight I should tuck you in." My beautiful 12-year-old boy.

3

Gordon Wakes Up

The doctors planned to keep Gordon in a medically induced coma for three days to allow his brain to begin recovering. They would bring him out occasionally just to see how he was responding—if he was responding—then put him back to sleep. When we arrived the next morning, we were told he was doing so well they were going to bring him out of the coma after just 24 hours.

Doing so well?? 24 hours, not 72? That little voice in the back of my head began to whisper, "Maybe we are going to be okay."

The nurse at the desk hit the button and the big doors to the Neuro-ICU swung open. We very tiptoed past all the other patients' rooms to get to Gordon's, the last room in the unit. Through each door we passed, I saw much older patients, most with bandages on their heads; no one was conscious.

The kids and I walked into Gordon's room. He was asleep, looking exactly as he had when the paramedics laid him on our bed and exactly as he had on the table in the ER. No bandages, just lots of tubes taped to his arms and hands. The machines monitoring his vitals hummed behind him.

He opened his eyes. I cried as quietly as I could. He closed his eyes. I held his hand. When he eventually opened his eyes again, I asked him if he knew who I was. After a moment, he

19

said in a raspy whisper, "Yes." That little voice in the back of my head wanted to start making happy noises.

The nurse began asking Gordon questions. His voice weak, Gordon tried to answer, but I could see in his expression that he was unsure of what was going on around him. He had a look on his face like he had walked into the wrong room and was trying to figure out where he had made the wrong turn. He moved his lips slightly, but made no sound. After a moment or two, his voice came out but it was more like breath than voice.

Rachel and Tommy stood on the other side of the hospital bed. The nurse asked Gordon if he had any children. He softly said, "No." Then she pointed to Rachel and Tommy and asked, "Who are they?" Gordon whispered, "Rachel and Tommy." That optimistic little voice in the back of my head was getting quieter. Gordon was saying yes and no, but he didn't really know what those words meant. What else did he not know?

For the few minutes Gordon could stay awake, I tried to get a handle on how the stroke had affected him. I told him that he had a stroke and was in the hospital. I asked him if he could move but he was too tired to respond. I told him he had really scared us and that we were happy he was awake. He smiled, or half smiled. Only the left side of Gordon's face moved. The right side of his face drooped and sagged. Motionless.

It began to dawn on me just how bad the stroke was. In those few minutes we had been together in the Neuro-ICU, I began to realize that Gordon's memory, his ability to speak and comprehend language, and the right side of his body all were affected.

The left side of the brain—the reasoning and speech-centric side—controls the right side of one's body. The right side of the brain—the visual and artistic side--controls the left.

When Gordon's left brain stroked, the right side of his body lost its connection with its command center and was completely limp. His voice was weak and his words were garbled. He wasn't sure who we were. The nurse asked him what year it was. Gordon mumbled something about the 1980s. She asked where he lived. He slowly whispered the name of a town in a different state. He was in very bad shape.

But what did that mean in the long-term? Were these issues temporary? I've seen lots of medical dramas on television and no one ever remains this bad off. As a matter of fact, on every medical drama, the patient is attentive, animated, and thanking the doctor on their way out of the hospital! They might be in a wheelchair, but only as a precaution.

What would our departure look like?

4

Recovering!

For the next three days, we went to the Neuro-ICU and although Gordon needed a lot of sleep, he was quite obviously recovering. He was moving his fingers and toes on his right side—weak, but moving! He was asking me questions about work and the appointments he had scheduled. His voice was weak and he was certainly not fully clear on all the things he wanted to talk about, but he was remembering and he was working through his lapses in memory and language.

These were good signs—wonderful signs! If he could keep this rate of recovery, Gordon was going to fully recover in a few months! That little voice in the back of my head was getting awfully optimistic, saying things like, "We are going to be OK! Gordon is going to be fine! This was just a nasty bump in the road!"

Then there was Gordon's appetite. I don't think there has ever been a time in Gordon's life where he has lost his appetite. Years before, Gordon had been having terrible abdominal pain and nausea and the doctor thought it might be appendicitis. He decided against appendicitis because Gordon was eating normally. It turned out it *was* appendicitis—his appetite was just stronger than the pain.

Lying in that ICU bed, Gordon was hungry. The nurse handed me a plate of waffles and told me to feed him.

It is funny—you don't think of only half your mouth or half your tongue or half your throat working—but that is exactly the way it was.

Gordon happily opened his mouth for the tasty bites and began to chew. Immediately, half-chewed food began spilling out of the right side of his mouth. He felt the waffles on the left side of his mouth but did not feel anything on his right side. Since he didn't remember he had a right side, this did not seem strange to him at all.

Nobody said anything. When he was done, the nurse instructed Gordon to place his finger in his mouth and fish out all the food stuck in his cheek. He was shocked to see all the chewed up food on his hand.

I laughed, the kids laughed, and Gordon laughed. It felt good. It felt normal. I started to relax, just a little more.

I wrote a blog to keep our friends and family updated with all that was happening. Each night, I wrote about the events of the day and read the sweet, supportive, caring notes people wrote to us. People were praying for us and offering to help if we needed help.

The notes that made me laugh and cry at the same time were recollections and observations of Gordon, his humor, his love, and his exuberance for life.

- *"I wonder if you [Gordon] remember how we first met. Tommy and you were walking home from school. You introduced yourself as Tommy's older brother."*

- *"...with a happy attitude like his you'll get through this ordeal in no time. I can't wait for the chicken fights in the pool this summer"* (from a 5th grader).

- *"I hardly know Gordon, but I do remember and my son remembers him from the pool. He remembered he was the nice man that would play with the kids and 'throw us really far!' in the pool."*

- *"Hope to see you walk on your hands this summer."*

- *"What is spring and summer without the sight of you and Jill walking the streets of Palisades in the early evening?"*

- *"I visited Gordon in the hospital today. When I asked him how he was doing, it was a classic Gordon response of 'Great!'"*

- *"I was able to spend 5 minutes with Gordon last night before visiting hours ended, and he looked good—in fact, fantastic, given that he had had a stroke just the day before! He was awake, focused, and smiling. He grabbed my hand with his left hand (plenty of strength there). He tried to talk but was unable. He nodded yes when I asked him if he wanted a pad of paper and a pen. He had difficulty writing (I'm sure that not being left-handed played some part in that), but he was still able to write that he loved Jill (I'm holding back tears right now thinking about it)."*

By the fourth day, Gordon was doing so well, they moved him out of Neuro-ICU and into the regular hospital. He was much too weak to walk, but his movement continued to revive and his thinking was sorting out as well. His work associate, Scott, came to visit and he and Gordon talked about Gordon's clients.

That lost look on Gordon's face when he first woke up was receding. His speech was broken, but coming back. His memory was foggy, but coming back. His right side was extremely weak, but coming back.

All indicators were positive for his recovery. The plan was to move to the rehab hospital on Day 5. By all accounts, Gordon was coming back at an amazing pace.

5

Rehab

Gordon was moved to the rehab hospital the next day. A lovely social worker named Ann coordinated Gordon's coverage with our insurance company. Gordon would have three weeks of inpatient rehabilitation, then in-home therapy for 60 visits. After that, we had 20 outpatient visits, which would bring us to the end of the year.

Nine months dedicated to recovery—I figured that was all we needed. Gordon was going to be back on his feet and ready to once again take on the world by then. Gordon was a little insulted that I thought it would take that long! He anticipated being back to work in six months, at the latest.

I told Gordon I was going to complete the long-term disability claim forms for insurance policies he had purchased many years before. He told me I was wasting my time—he would be better before the 6-month waiting period expired. I started working on them anyway, just in case the full nine months I anticipated was correct.

Gordon's roommate at rehab was a soft-spoken, elderly gentleman named Roger. Roger had been a banker in his earlier days but was now recovering from his second aneurysm in six months. He was toward the end of his therapy and provided a glimpse of what recovery might look like for Gordon. Roger walked and talked and cautiously functioned quite well. He was a lovely man. We liked Roger.

Gordon was very tired but very excited about rehab. By the time he completed his second day of rehab, he was exercising both arms and standing on both legs. Gordon loves a challenge, so in a funny way rehab was right up his alley. He received two physical, occupational and speech therapy treatments each day. When I asked him which he liked best, he said characteristically, "All of them."

Now that little voice in my head was becoming more confident that, while we were going to have a tough six to nine months, we would then be back to normal. Only seven days separated my shocking conversation with the woman in the white lab coat and this rehab experience. It was miraculous. How far we had come!

6

But Then...

Day 8. Terrible, crushing, shocking Day 8. The evening before, Gordon had become very sleepy—more than usual— and then had an excruciating night with a severe headache. Now, the morning of Day 8, he could stay awake for less than a minute at a time. All movement on his right side stopped. He struggled to form words. He remembered nothing. They did a CT scan, and MRI, and an MRA of his brain, but found no obvious bleeding, just the same swelling as before.

What happened? The standard response from every medical professional was, "Every stroke is different." That standard response, while true, is maddeningly unhelpful. Seriously, just say "I don't know" or "more brain is dying due to the initial stroke" or "All those clots that were left behind are doing their damage now" or "It's the swelling"—something! Anything! Instead, stoic faces gave no answers.

Every stroke is different. One doctor changed it up a little. She said "Once you've seen one stroke, you've seen one stroke." Yup, just as helpful.

After recovering extremely well in those first few days, Gordon was getting dramatically worse. He couldn't stay awake during his therapy sessions, but we dragged him to them anyway.

I thought he should be re-admitted to the regular hospital to find out what was wrong, but that idea was never considered. Why not? We had only 21 days of inpatient rehabilitation insurance and we were wasting them because Gordon was now incapable of participating.

Hope drained out of me. I never heard from that optimistic little voice in my head, ever again.

Nights were particularly awful. At night, the headaches would start. Gordon reacted badly to the pain medications, and the sleep aids knocked him out for the entire next day so there wasn't much the doctor could give him. Each morning when I came into the room, I would ask his roommate, Roger, how Gordon's night went. Roger always reported truthfully. His answers ranged from "not good" to "His were the cries of a dying man."

I don't know how he did it, but Gordon didn't get depressed. Maybe it was because the left side of his brain was damaged —the side that considers the implications of such events. Then again, my left brain worked just fine. These events and their implications were like monoliths in front of me, stark, obvious, and overwhelming.

I began to allow my mind to wander. I began to fantasize about dying myself. What a relief it would be to just die and be done with all this. I started wishing a bus would run over me. I knew I couldn't step in front of a bus and die; I had kids who needed me. Then again, if a bus innocently ran me over and I died—great! It wouldn't be my fault, but I could still be dead. It sounded so good. Life was too hard. Facing each moment, not to mention each day, was too much.

People say God never gives you more than you can handle. I have pondered this statement for some time now, and respectfully note that this promise is often taken out of context. The proper context is regarding temptation, not adversity. I think He sometimes gives us far more than we can handle, just to make sure we know we are just not that powerful, not that capable, not that strong. He can give us so much burden that all we can do is drop to our knees and cry out, "I can't make it! I can't carry this load! I am weak. I am helpless."

The crushing weight of the burden handed to me put me face down on the floor, begging for mercy. I was in complete and utter surrender. I waved my white flag to my Creator and Savior. It was time to stop making plans, stop anticipating, stop thinking I had any control. It was time to trust Him.

I thought of that rather cliché story of the two sets of footprints in the sand—one set belonged to Jesus and the other to a man. At one point, the man faces challenges and notices, looking back, that during the difficult time, there was only one set of footprints. He questions Jesus about why He left the man during his struggle. Jesus responds "Those are my footprints. I was carrying you." That was me! I needed to be carried. My strength was gone. I began to ask Jesus to carry me down this path I could not walk down by myself. Every morning and every night, I handed Him my worries. I waited to see where He would carry me.

A new morning routine quickly settled into place. After I got the kids off to school, I dug into the mountain of insurance forms and other paperwork sitting on our kitchen counter. Payments from Gordon's two small disability policies purchased nearly 25 years ago would kick in after six months, but I had to do the paperwork now. Pages and pages of forms needed to be completed. Five years of tax documents needed to be copied and mailed to both companies. On top of that, it was now early April and taxes were due April 15th. I needed to deal with that too. Then medical bills started arriving.

After spending all afternoon at the rehab hospital with Gordon, I worked in the evenings, trying to figure out our accounting program. Between manual bill paying, electronic bill paying, and automatic bill paying, I was up to my eyeballs in the practical side of losing my partner. I spent hours searching through paper and computer files, looking for passwords, account numbers, and due dates.

The financial realities of our situation weighed heavily on me. Gordon was an independent consultant—there was no company structure to work within. There was no job waiting for him when he recovered. There were no HR people with experience in this area waiting for my call. There was no employer-sponsored comprehensive health insurance plan to cover most of the expenses. We were on our own with a high deductible health plan. It was up to me to figure it all out.

We worked hard and saved as much as we could, but we were nowhere near prepared for this. How can anyone be prepared for this? Thursday, March 27th, we had nearly $50,000 in our checking account. Now, here we were in the second week in April with the full medical deductible paid, plus state and federal taxes, and our account was nearly empty. No more income was coming—only bills.

One evening, after everyone else was asleep, I walked around my dark house and said goodbye to everything we owned. I imagined the day strangers would walk through my house, buying what they liked and criticizing what they didn't. I thought about the few things I would need to keep.

I envisioned locking the door behind me for the last time—
this house where we raised our children, marked their height
on their bedroom door jams, dreamed of our future together,
and celebrated Christmases and birthdays.

Somehow, saying goodbye made me feel better. I felt
released. The longer I clung to "the stuff," the harder it was
going to be to get through what seemed inevitable: We were
going to lose everything.

I was exhausted. I wasn't sleeping well at night and I was too
stressed to eat. My children were 12 and 14, tough years
anyway, looking to me to assure them and take care of them.
I did my best to provide calm stability for them, trying to
keep their routines as normal as possible. I thought back,
longingly, to my mundane life. I missed those ordinary
nights where we sat in front of the TV and I complained that
we were wasting our time watching stupid shows. Now I
longed for the ordinariness of life; I longed for our routine,
silly stuff.

Then again, though God may have given me more than I
could handle, He certainly didn't abandon me. In my time of
utter surrender, a small army of people was gathering to
bring reinforcements.

As I sat in the hospital, trying to comprehend what was
happening around me, friends and family were mobilizing,
organizing communications, food, and support for us. While
I was busy taking care of business, friends and family *really*
stepped up.

- Keith and Teri had a beautiful banister built so
  Gordon could hold on with his left hand and get up
  the stairs to the bedroom.

- The neighbors helped move furniture so that Gordon could have an extra bed on the main floor.

- Brent installed grab bars and bathroom equipment for Gordon's safety.

- A list of men volunteered to come over at night to help Gordon climb the stairs if we needed them.

- Bill spent hours with me, teaching me to how to use our accounting software.

- Wendy cleaned our house.

- Doug mowed my lawn and then Cyrus sent his gardeners to handle the whole yard.

- Kate lent us an additional wheelchair so we could have one upstairs and one downstairs.

- Another friend, also named Jill, started a list of people who wanted to help with meals. That list immediately booked out 3 months.

- Joyce, a recently retired doctor and casual acquaintance, offered to come alongside us through this journey and help us navigate the medical world. She was our own private doctor-consultant-friend, free of charge.

- Molly opened a bank account for us and got the word out to anyone who might want to help us financially. When I stopped by the bank to check the account there was nearly $6,000 in it.

As time went on, other miraculous things revealed themselves. Only three months before Gordon's stroke,

OHSU had been added to our health plan. No notice had been sent by the insurance company; it happened quietly. Because of this fact, we would be charged in-network fees and there was a limit to our out-of-pocket dollar obligation. It was still going to be expensive, but nowhere near what it could have cost us.

Fifteen years before, Gordon had made a small investment in a company in California. We had for the most part forgotten about it. The company sold that year and out of nowhere, a check for $20,000 showed up. Incredible? No—miraculous.

There were some funny moments at the rehab hospital. After ten days of not shaving, my Italian husband began to look like a disabled wolf man. My brother, Brent, brought his electric razor to the hospital so Gordon could shave safely. Even in his stupor, Gordon took one look at the electric razor, knew it would never cut his beard, and said "No."

Trying to be as upbeat as possible, we encouraged Gordon to give it a whirl. So he tried it. Gordon was right—not even the finest German-made electric razor could bring down those Mediterranean-inspired whiskers. Now he looked like a disabled wolf man with two little shaved spots on his cheeks.

In his stupor, with only his left hand (he is, unfortunately, right handed) he shaved with a cheap, plastic razor. By the time he finished, Gordon had so many cuts on his face you would have thought he lost a knife fight. To make it even worse, he was on blood thinners, so he bled for days.

7

Recovering—Take 2

We finally started seeing improvement in his last week in the rehab hospital. Gordon started to get the hang of using his cane to take several steps. He could name three fruits in speech therapy and he figured out what a red triangle was.

Bits and pieces of the old Gordon were coming back. We were discussing telephones and telephone numbers and I reminded him of ours. Gordon, Mr. Goal Setter, said he was going to try to make a call and see if he could dial a phone. I was skeptical since only the day before, I had explained to him what phones were and how to use them. Sure enough, after I had finished the dinner dishes that evening, the phone rang. Gordon's whispery voice was on the other end. He called just to say hi.

The highlight of those last days at the hospital was being pushed around the neighborhood in his wheelchair by Rachel. At 14 years old, Rachel stood 5 feet 1 inches tall, and weighed 85 pounds after a big meal. She would push and push and Gordon would say things like "more" and "faster." He just loved being outside, enjoying the breeze, listening to the noises, and watching people.

He was quite a sight: half paralyzed, barely able to speak, partially bald (at one point half his hair fell out), looking around as if he had never seen a tree before.

He remembered that his favorite ice cream was chocolate mint, but he didn't remember that it cost money. He didn't know what he looked like and he didn't care. He just loved being with our family and friends who might visit. He just sat in the wheelchair and smiled with the left side of his face while the world went on around him.

Gordon was approaching his release date. One of the boxes to be checked on the release forms was for Gordon and me to meet individually with the psychiatrist. I had never met with a psychiatrist before so I was a little curious what would happen. What would the office look like? Would it be a warm, wooden bookcase lined office with a comfy couch, just like on TV? Nope. It was a small, white, generic office with a couple of chairs lined up against the wall.

The psychiatrist asked a few questions about me and our family, trying to gauge where we were in understanding what had happened to us. She asked about our support system—family, friends. She gave me a general description of what the next few years would look like. There was no optimism, no pessimism, no emotion at all. Just the likely reality of our life going forward.

I didn't cry. I didn't hold my head in my hands asking, "What is going to happen to us?" I did not want a prescription for antidepressants. I think it was my first day with my game face on. Gordon was coming home. I was going to be his caregiver. Life as we knew it was over. I was responsible for everything. I needed to be sharp. I needed to be ready for the changes coming our way.

Then it was Gordon's turn with the psychiatrist. When I retrieved him from her office, he was very upset. She had told him he wouldn't work for at least two years and when he protested, she asked him questions about his work. He had no answers for her.

As I rolled him back to his room, Gordon said, "I don't know what I do. Do you know?" I explained it to him. He nodded like he understood, but as the seconds ticked by, he forgot what I said.

As I helped Gordon back into his bed, I explained again, and again, and he nodded in understanding. Within moments, Gordon had that same puzzled look on his face.

Slowly, he began to realize the full impact of what happened to him. Up to this moment, living in his right brain, he hadn't fully understood the seriousness of the stroke and had not fully grasped the long-term implications.

Lying in his bed, Gordon asked, as a child asks his mother: "What happened to me?" It was a terrible, terrible moment for me and for Gordon. Yet I believe it marked the true beginning of his recovery. The first step toward fixing a problem is acknowledging it.

In those final days at the rehab hospital, some activities were kind of comical, while others were truly eye opening. Gordon had to learn how to go to the bathroom by himself...well, almost by himself. I needed to be there to help him and do it in a way that was not humiliating or embarrassing for either of us.

What about showering? What about dressing? He needed help with all these things. With only one functioning hand, he couldn't cut up his food, zip his jacket, or tie his shoes. I cut his nails for him.

He was in a wheelchair so I had to learn how to get him in and out of the car safely. That crazy-heavy wheelchair had to be folded, lifted in and out of the car, and prepared for him.

Then some scary stuff: If Gordon fell and nobody was around, what was his plan to get up? What should he do? What if he couldn't find help? How does a half-paralyzed man get up? He was on blood thinners—what if he started bleeding and couldn't stop? Even worse, what if he fell and began bleeding internally?

The left side of his body was going to have to do all the work while Gordon's right side hung there, getting in the way. I was going to have to help with all of it and I was going to have to do it with a smile on my face and an encouraging tone in my voice. It was going to be like managing a 160-pound baby, maybe forever.

8

Going Home

When our three weeks of rehab were up, it was time to leave the hospital for good. As I drove, I continued to envision Jesus carrying me through the sand, while Gordon looked out the window in wonder, like a dog with the car window open, thrilled to be going home.

Here is a funny thing about Gordon's brain at that time. He didn't know what year it was, where we lived, what he did for a living—nothing! Yet he remembered gas prices. In April 2008, gas prices doubled from $2 to $4 a gallon. We passed a gas station and out of his fatigued, foggy brain, Gordon clearly said, "Wow! Gas went up!" Seriously? You don't remember your children, but you remember gas prices?

Earlier, I lamented that the medical community's response to every recovery question is "Every stroke is different." Now I will tell you the good side of that statement. There may be no encouragement, but there is also no discouragement. The neurosurgeon's parting words to us were, "I don't know how much you will get back. All I can say is that those who want it most recover best."

Together, we wanted it most. We wanted full recovery. We wanted our life back. Gordon wanted to work again, wanted to walk unassisted, wanted to have complete conversations. He wanted to play golf and he wanted to play with our kids.

We took the doctor's words to heart and decided, there and then, that we were going to do whatever we could to get back his abilities. The challenge was clear and there were no rules or limitations.

And so began the long journey of recovery—more of a slog, really. Our time in the hospital was highly structured with professionals around us at all times. Now we were home, figuring out what to do next.

A new set of therapists came to the house to help Gordon with speech, walking, and using his upper body. Everything he did or tried to do required so much concentration and effort that he would need to sleep often. His brain was working so hard to rewire that he slept 15 hours a day. I set up a bed in what was the dining room so he could avoid the stairs to our bedroom during the day.

When therapists weren't with him, I worked with Gordon, trying to get his right side to respond. For hours, day after day, week after week, month after month, and year after year we worked together, going through the exercises left by the therapists and trying to get his brain to rewire and reconnect.

The brain needs time to remake those lost connections, and visualization and imagination play a big part in that process. When no muscles were responding, I did the exercises for Gordon while he watched. As I moved his arm, wrist, and fingers, we talked about how it would look if he were able to do it without me. He imagined what it would feel like if he moved his hand. I rubbed, tickled, and tapped his skin so his brain would acknowledge feeling in his paralyzed limb. We placed his chair in front of a mirror and I lifted his shoulders at the same time so he could see both sides of his body working together.

Even five years later, when Gordon was working on opening his right hand, we talked about how it would look if he could lift one finger at a time.

It was a test of patience, diligence, and creativity, trying to make each day enjoyable and fun, even though improvement was slow and sometimes nonexistent.

If we could get even a flicker from a muscle, we would focus on that muscle and try to build strength and hope that the next muscle would eventually flicker and do the same. We celebrated the tiniest improvement and encouraged each other through the dry spells.

Gordon's ability—or inability—to think and speak clearly probably has brought the most laughter and teasing in our house. Rachel was the first to play therapeutic games with Gordon and test out what he could do. Her job was to describe an image on a therapy sheet and Gordon had to guess what she was describing. When that didn't go so well, we decided to switch—Gordon would describe and she would guess.

Gordon thought he was *amazing* at this game because he would say a few words and Rachel quickly guessed every one right! He didn't realize he was saying the word rather than describing it, and she was just saying the word back to him. For example, Gordon said, "Store that sells books."

She said "Bookstore" and looked at Gordon suspiciously, trying to decide if Gordon was just messing with her, which would have been normal for pre-stroke Gordon. But he wasn't messing with her. He truly thought he was simply giving great clues. When it dawned on her what was going on, she gave me that Jack Benny look and we both started to laugh. When she told Gordon what he was doing, my sweet husband started to laugh too. What a good sport!

Gordon worked on elementary school-level math worksheets, relearning addition and subtraction. He picked it up quickly, so I got flashcards to help him relearn multiplication tables. After his shower at night, Gordon often sat in the recliner in the bedroom and I sat in his wheelchair facing him and showed him flashcards. Slowly but surely, he began to answer correctly. Within a few weeks he had regained his basic understanding of math—except for his 7's. For some reason, he just could not remember his 7's, and still can't today. Thank goodness for calculators.

Every now and then, after those first few weeks of having Gordon home again, the realization of my new life struck me like a knife through the heart. Gordon's life was now my life. He was helpless without me.

In pre-stroke life, I went to the gym on Monday and Thursday mornings. I went on walks with friends through the streets of our town. I volunteered at the kids' schools. I was on the board of our National Charity League chapter, which I also helped start. I answered phones at our church a few mornings each month. I cleaned, washed, cooked, baked, mowed, weeded, edged, and pruned at home. Gordon and I had a clear division of labor: he earned money and paid the bills, and I did everything else. It worked for us. We both liked working hard and we both felt fulfilled.

But now, that life was over. I cancelled the gym membership immediately—no money for that luxury. I couldn't leave Gordon alone, so my interaction with the outside world was mostly limited to therapists and the nice people at the grocery store. I had been active and involved in the community. That was over.

I tried to sneak in moments of normalcy, but there was no getting around the fact that nothing was the same. All I held as normal was no longer our normal.

I didn't even take pictures. This was not what I wanted to memorialize in photographs. During Gordon's hospital stay, he had lost 20 pounds and now looked pale and gaunt. He was still working on getting the right side of his face to respond, but for now, it sagged like melted wax. The back and left side of his head was still bald with little patches of fuzz beginning to grow. His right arm dangled awkwardly, even with the brace designed to hold his shoulder joint in its socket. Add to that image his cut up face from shaving. When he stood, he leaned heavily on his cane. No, this was not what I wanted to remember. It was upsetting to me, but I was quite sure it would be even more upsetting to Gordon.

Gordon was now my life. I had to make peace with that. If I couldn't, I knew only misery lay ahead for me and for my family. Fighting the facts certainly wouldn't change them and feeling sorry for myself openly and aggressively would help no one. Fantasizing about getting run over by the city bus had to stop. I was welcome to cry in my closet by myself, but ultimately I had to suck it up. Gordon and the kids needed me to fill that massive gap in our lives the stroke had created. And I did cry. I cried every day for months.

The more I longed for my old life, the clearer it became that I had to change.

It took a lot of sad days, but I finally got it through my thick head that surrender was my only option.

It was time to find out what it really meant to put God first—not my dreams, not my aspirations, not the way things used to be, not even my concept of reality. Everything belongs to God and He is in control. Not me.

Admitting my own powerlessness was hard. I leaned heavily on God's words of faithful love, the words that acknowledge our need for Him in our dark hours.

> *Call to me and I will answer you and tell you great and unsearchable things you do not know (Jeremiah 33:3 NIV).*
>
> *I am praying to you because I know you will answer, O God. Bend down and listen as I pray (Psalm 17:6 NLT).*
>
> *Don't worry about anything; instead, pray about everything. Tell God what you need, and thank Him for all He has done (Philippians 4:6 NLT).*
>
> *Don't let your hearts be troubled. Trust in God, and trust also in me (John 14:1 NTL).*

9

Who Am I and How Did I Get Here?

Different events in our lives take on differing levels of significance over time. As we look back at certain occurrences in our past, what seemed very important at the time may eventually reveal itself to be just "something that happened" if we remember it at all. Then again, seemingly everyday experiences may have far reaching implications in the building of our character or in the course of our lives.

What experiences brought me to this place at this time? What prepared me, if you could call me prepared, to face this challenge? Who had God prepared me to be in order to carry this load that dropped on me and my family? Who am I and how did I get here?

I am an Iowa farm girl. I had the good fortune of spending my first eight years on a Mid-Western farm with my parents and two older brothers. For us kids, the farm was like a giant playground with few actual toys. Who needed toys? We had a farm to play with. Then again, our playground had few guard rails or entirely safe spaces. We learned to play with risk and consequence as natural playmates.

We had a barn with a haymow. As we climbed the rough-hewn ladder nailed to the wall up to the haymow, we could hear birds, mice, and cats scurrying due to our disruption. We climbed the tall piles of hay, swung from a rope, and landed in other piles of hay. There were big holes in the floor where my dad easily dropped hay down to the cattle in the barn below, so paying attention to where we walked was essential if we didn't want to make that same drop.

We had an old chicken house that hadn't housed chickens in decades. Instead, it had become a multi-use structure. While Dad used it to store field equipment, my brothers and I used it for other things. It served as a backstop for missed baseball pitches. The roof line was low so we could climb on top of old discarded equipment in back, get on the roof and shimmy up to the wind vane on top. Once we made it to the peak, we could hide, throw things, or even slide off—fall off, really— into the snow in winter. When my brothers stole Dad's cigarettes, the chicken house roof was where we went to light them up.

We had a corn crib—a tall cinderblock building with a conveyer belt system that transported the field corn from the trailers up into tall storage areas at harvest time. All year long, this corn would be used to feed the cattle. For the boys and me, filling the storage cribs was like a carnival ride with no safety belts.

Dad drove the tractor into the corn crib and parked the trailer at the conveyer belt. We kids climbed into the trailer filled with corn and held on tight. Dad flipped the switch that elevated the front of the trailer while he opened the trap door at the low end. The boys and I pushed the corn out through the trap door as we slid, rolled, and crawled in silly laughter along the steep slope of the trailer. We dangled from the trailer's mid beam, always careful not to fall through the trap door or lose a shoe in the process. When the trailer was empty, we waited for the next full trailer and did it all again.

The corn crib had a manual elevator to take one person at a time to the top of the 3-story storage cribs. The rider stood on a small, open platform and had to understand how to use counter weights along with the rope and pulley system if he wanted the elevator to travel both up *and* down. I watched men ride the elevator up into the darkness and back down again, deftly manipulating the ropes, pulleys, and weights. I never understood those darned counter weights so I never got to ride. The elevator remained a mystery to me.

Behind the corn crib, a pile of corn cobs waited, excellent for throwing at each other. They are lightweight and fit perfectly in a kid's hand so anyone can throw one. The great thing about corn cobs is that you never had to wonder if you had been hit. Those cobs were so hard and rough, it was impossible to have a corn cob fight and not come out with slightly less blood than when you went in.

The first time I ever shot a gun was at the corncob pile. I was six years old. Dad shoved some cans into the pile, put me tightly in front of him so my back was against his chest, and showed me how to aim the rifle. When I pulled the trigger, he absorbed the recoil. He let me shoot until I hit a can. My guess is he got tired of waiting, aimed for me, and let me pull the trigger.

Guns are a part of life and death on a farm. Sick animals have to be put down. Predatory animals need to be eliminated. If a feral animal was lurking, Dad could place a loaded rifle just inside the back door for quick access without worrying about us touching the gun. From examining those shot-up cans in the corncob pile to burying those shot-up animals, the consequences of a gunshot were very clear to us kids. No one messed with the rifle.

There was always something to do down at the crick—that's right—the crick. We trudged through the pasture to get to the murky, muddy water. There was fishing for bullheads in the summer, ice skating in winter, and catching guppies in a jar before the ice got too thick. We had an artesian well that fed into the crick. A metal pipe stuck out of the ground and the slow, steady stream of perfect water trickled out. We drank from it as did every other animal that passed by, I am sure.

We chased the horses, avoided the cattle, played with our many cats, climbed our maple tree (which we also tried to chop down with a croquet mallet) and rode our bikes. I don't think there was a better place to be a child.

My brothers were old enough to work on the farm. This is where the idyllic life takes a turn. Before the corn crib could be filled with newly harvested corn, anything remaining of the old harvest had to be cleaned out. The boys were small enough to fit into the rat-infested crawlspaces of the corn crib. Dad tied rope around their pant legs at the ankles, closing them off so that no critters could run up inside. Then he sent them crawling into the crawlspaces with brooms and a flashlight to clean out the old grain, along with any dead animals they might find.

They mowed our large lawn, our grandfather's large lawn and our aunt and uncle's large lawn. They once spent an entire hot, humid, Iowa summer painting all the fences on the farm. They "walked beans," walking up and down every row of soybeans with a hoe, removing weeds by hand. It may not sound like a big job until you understand that the field and therefore each row was a half mile long. I walked beans only once, and it was hot, dirty, exhausting work.

My mother took care of us kids and our old farmhouse, the same house where my father was born. She cooked three large meals every day, raised a large garden of vegetables and a second, equally large garden of flowers. There is no rest for a farm wife. She sewed our clothes, canned our vegetables, and I am guessing went nearly crazy being stuck out in the middle of nowhere with three active kids and work that never ended.

Dad raised cattle, corn, and soybeans. Regardless of the weather—hot, cold, humid, snowing, sleeting, raining or pleasant—cattle need to be fed twice a day, seven days a week. Every morning before dawn, he loaded the trailer with grain he had stored from the previous year's crop, fired up the tractor, and filled the feed bunks while cattle waited for breakfast. Every evening the ritual was the same for their dinner. The rest of the day was spent in the fields or doing other farm work. On the really pleasant evenings, he let me ride on the tractor with him and pull the lever that released the feed. I loved that.

In the summer the cattle were let loose to graze in the pasture until all the tall grass looked like a closely mowed lawn. When the grass was eaten and it was time to bring the cattle back inside the fences, my cousin came over, saddled up the horses, and helped round up the herd. The horses were so smart, and so excited to do the rounding up, they didn't need anyone on their backs to get the job done. Then again, the men enjoyed it too much to just let the horses have all the fun.

Our tiny town of 500 people was populated with generations of immigrant families, mostly German. Typical for small towns, everyone knew everyone, which can be both a blessing and a curse. No one locked their doors. I don't think we had a key to our house. The only traffic signal was a blinking red light that anyone could turn off by holding down a switch bolted to the traffic pole. There were two churches in town, a Methodist Church and a Lutheran Church. Every family picked one and every family attended on Sunday.

The life of a farmer is a life filled with risk. There were only two paydays each year—the day we sold our livestock and the day we sold our crops. If prices were low that year, we might lose money after all our investment and hard work. If a bad storm blew through, the crops might be ruined and we were down to one paycheck that year. What if there was no rain? What if there was too much rain? What if sickness broke out in the livestock? A farmer could do everything right and still end up with nothing.

As a result, my parents were extremely frugal, always preparing for the worst. Spending any money at all was stressful. They went out to dinner only twice a year—once for Mother's Day and once for their anniversary. The Mother's Day dinner barely even counts as "going out" because dinner was really lunch and it was at the town cafe and us kids got to go too. I guess it counted for my mother—no cooking and no dishes was a treat.

We went to "the city" once a year for clothes shopping. We bought coats and jeans and things we needed for the winter. I had an older cousin who gave me her hand-me-downs so I got a few extra things to wear. Making do with what we had was an art we perfected. Since most people around us were just as cheap as we were, it seemed normal. We didn't know any other way.

For a child, it was the perfect setting. We were free to roam, experiment, work as a team, amuse ourselves, get in trouble, injure ourselves, fall, fail, fight, succeed, discover, and have real responsibility. We watched our parents work hard to achieve tangible results. I consider myself blessed to be an Iowa farm girl. My childhood gave me a foundation of faith, resourcefulness, resilience, confidence, and a very clear understanding of consequences.

But for risk-averse people like Mom and Dad, a different life called to them. A stable, predictable job with a paycheck, vacation time, and set hours suited them much better than the farm life. When I was eight years old, we packed up our belongings and moved to San Diego, California.

We lived on a dead-end street in a house that backed up to miles and miles of open hills. Motorcycle and horse trails went on, seemingly forever. No more green cornfields and black, loamy soil. Now we looked at sandy trails, sagebrush, cactus and a big dead tree in the distance where the hawks perched, looking for creepy reptiles to eat. It was a different kind of beauty and a different kind of adventure. I ran through the hills with my new friends and quickly adjusted to my new life. We all loved San Diego.

Dad got a job at an equipment rental company. He was the Yard Man. He swept the asphalt lot and washed the equipment—earth movers, tractors, bulldozers, etc. It was the bottom rung of the corporate ladder but he didn't mind at all. His eye was on the branch manager's job and he knew that hard work, integrity, and being a quick learner would most likely get him to his goal. Without a college education, he had no credentials to move him up that ladder. He would have to earn each rung with hard work.

Within a few years, Dad was the branch manager. A few years after that, he was promoted to the corporate office—the furthest he could go without that college degree. Mom and Dad were happy and learning to enjoy life. They went to their favorite restaurant every Sunday night. They had good friends and socialized regularly. My brothers were striding into adulthood and I was in college and loving it. Things seemed to be going our way and we appreciated it.

Dad died suddenly of a heart attack when I was 19, leaving my mother devastated and alone. My parents had been high school sweethearts and married soon after graduation. Most of their lives were spent together. With my dad gone, my mother was 43 years old and facing life on her own for the first time. She had a high school education and no employment experience. Her entire identity was that of wife and mother. I am the youngest child and I was in college so there wasn't even a child home for her to mother. Her vocabulary was built around the pronouns "us" and "we," not "I" and "me." Her identity was pulled out from under her and she was struggling to find her footing. She was sad.

It didn't occur to me that I was awfully young to lose my father. I figured that being 19 years old, I wasn't a child anymore. After all, at 19 my mother was married, had a baby and lived isolated on a farm in the middle of nowhere. I was in college and had only to take care of myself—how hard could that be? I had always been fairly independent and was used to not having much. I was going to have to figure out how to pay for school and rent and food without letting my grades slip. I knew how to do that. I had been working at various jobs since I was 15.

Two years later, in the fall of my senior year of college, Mom called and told me she was remarrying and I was thrilled for her. She was never meant to be alone, so if she could find happiness and companionship in a new man, I was happy for her. Her new husband's job took him to remote places around the world for years at a time. After the wedding she would be going with him. They left the U.S. after Christmas. She spent the next decade traveling the world with her husband, living a life that she had never dreamed possible for herself.

I took Mom's leaving as a vote of confidence in me. If she had been afraid I could not make it on my own, she never would have left. Denying herself a life full of adventure just because I was afraid to be alone would have been unacceptable to me. My parents hadn't raised sissies. I had all the tools I needed to take care of myself and establish my own life. I was free to make my own choices—good or bad—and deal with the consequences. I was free to be afraid; I just couldn't let fear get in my way.

I needed a strategy. I figured I could go one of two ways: (1) get married as soon as possible so I wouldn't have to deal with life alone or (2) embrace being alone. If I picked the first one, I could find shelter in marriage and trust that the man I chose would take care of me, protect me, and always be there for me. If I picked the second one, I could establish myself in a career, stretch my comfort zone, and prove to myself that I could make it in this world no matter what came my way.

In Option One the solution was all about me and what I could receive: find someone to take care of me, serve me, make me feel safe.

In Option Two the solution was all about what I could offer: competence, ability, partnership.

The path of my life was going to be determined by my strategy, and my strategy hinged upon these very different choices.

I chose the second one.

Looking forward to graduation, with no home to go home to, no money in my account and student loans to pay, I was what one might describe as "highly motivated" to work.

In the spring of my senior year I went to every job interview I could get through the university's career counseling office and it paid off. College graduation was on a Sunday. I started my first full-time job on Monday.

I worked, shared an apartment, paid my bills, and saved what money I could. I changed jobs nearly every year in order to advance my career and to broaden my experience and knowledge. I joined Toastmasters to improve my presentation skills and expand my professional network. I worked long hours. Five years after graduation, when I was 27 years old, I took my first vacation day.

Looking back, nothing seems accidental. Life was not easy, but its satisfaction was great. It made me capable and strong.

10

We Meet

That Gordon and I ever even met is an unlikely story steeped in divine direction.

It was 1989. I was 29 years old, living in Los Angeles with my dear friend Jane, and working as a real estate consultant for a large accounting firm. I worked long hours and traveled for my job, sometimes for months at a time. I had always known I eventually wanted to be married and have a family, but I hadn't felt ready for that step. If I didn't feel ready, there was no way I was going to force it to happen just because I was approaching 30. I had things to accomplish before I made that commitment.

Jane and I had become great friends with Dave, our neighbor down the hall. Dave and I were both from Iowa so he and I had that immediate bond that good Mid-Western farm folks have. Jane is that wonderful person who makes everyone feel welcome and important. The three of us were inseparable. We spent all our free time together, laughing, eating, drinking, and going on walks. Whatever we did, we did together.

One day, Dave told us his friend named Gordon was coming to LA for business. Dave encouraged him to stay for the weekend—he knew these two girls—and have some fun.

Gordon asked if he was assigned to a specific girl and Dave said yes...Jane.

Gordon's trip was a few weeks away and he didn't want his weekend with Jane to feel awkward so he telephoned her right away. He told her he would call every day so by the time he arrived they would already know each other.

Jane loved it. Every evening Gordon called and from my room I could hear her giggling and chatting with her future date. As the day of his arrival approached, Jane nervously asked if we could go shopping. She wanted some new outfits for the big weekend.

When the big day arrived, Jane was bursting with excitement and looked adorable in her new clothes. Dave and Gordon walked into our apartment and Gordon looked at me and said, "Are you Jane?" (Gordon later confided that the only picture he had seen of me before we met was of me sleeping in the backseat of a car. The picture was less than flattering so he was expecting me to be more of a Quasimodo-like character.) Once we got the names and identities straightened out, we were off on our weekend of fun and non-stop activity.

We had a great time. We ate Moroccan food with our hands. We walked through Santa Monica and Venice Beach. We lied to Gordon and told him Six Flags was closed so we wouldn't have to ride those giant roller coasters ... and he believed us. We watched movies. We laughed and we laughed and we laughed. With the four of us altogether, I made sure I focused more on Dave than Gordon. Gordon was Jane's date and I didn't want to intrude in any way.

Gordon and Jane seemed to be having a good time but they were clearly not a match. Jane liked polite gentlemen who wooed women at a slow pace. Gordon was gregarious and aggressive and there was nothing slow about his pace. Seeing them together made me think of the old Warner Brothers cartoons with Pepé Le Pew, the amorous skunk and the poor black cat with the white stripe painted down her back. Thinking she was just like him, Pepé was always pursuing the cat, while the cat was doing her best to deflect his advances. That image pretty much sums up Gordon and Jane that weekend.

As for me, I always liked aggressive men! I liked the confidence they exuded and I liked that I always knew where they stood on anything. Clear, concise, and action-oriented— that was my kind of man.

Jane took Gordon to the airport late Sunday afternoon. Afterward, she walked back into the apartment, dropped her purse, and lay down on the living room floor, exhausted. Just before she fell into a deep sleep, she said, "Oh, Jill. He should have been with you."

Jane was sleeping so deeply that she didn't even wake up when the phone rang later that evening. It was Gordon calling to thank us for a great time. The funny thing was that he never asked to speak to Jane. He and I talked instead. From that day on, we spoke on the phone every day. Eleven months later, we were married. Jane was one of my bridesmaids.

11

We Marry

Our life together was an adventure from the beginning.
We lived in the Bay Area where Gordon was a partner in a
startup telesales company. Starting a company is difficult,
time intensive, and expensive. Utilities, rent, insurance,
expenses, and employee salaries all must be paid first with
the revenue earned in order to keep the business running. If
there is any money left over, then the partners get paid. If
there is no money left over, the partners do not get paid.

Gordon hadn't drawn a salary in over six months and had
racked up substantial credit card debt. Having sold all his
assets to start the company and not receiving any income, his
only option had been to charge all his expenses to multiple
credit cards. With high interest rates being charged on the
cards and the balances ever increasing, he was only making
the minimum payments.

Gordon had been very honest with me before the wedding
that he was heavily in debt and that it would be a long time
before the company would be profitable. He assured me that
he would never stop working to succeed and provide us with
the good things in life. He had given me the option of
backing out of the wedding with no hard feelings—he knew
this was a difficult situation to come into and he would
understand if this was not the life I wanted.

I didn't back out. I loved Gordon and I loved his work ethic, his honesty, and his sincerity in honoring my feelings. Ours felt like a "God ordained" relationship. That we had even met was against huge odds. Our relationship was completely honest and close from the first day we talked. I had no doubt that Gordon was the man God intended for me to marry. Our life wasn't going to be easy but I trusted God's choice for me. We would figure out the money part together.

We came up with a plan. I would get a good job and pay all the bills. Any money Gordon received would all go to paying off his debts. We estimated it would take three years. We stuck to the plan and achieved the goal in half the expected time. I have never seen anyone so excited to get to $0 as Gordon was, 18 months later. The day he paid off his last credit card was the day he happily took over the bill paying responsibility. I happily relinquished it to him.

Being the wife of an entrepreneur isn't easy for a non-risk taker like me. I like safe, well thought out action, and a general idea of potential outcomes. I think several steps ahead and work to ensure that I am prepared and ready for whatever may come. I am always in the correct lane in traffic so I am ready for the next turn. I prefer no surprises when it comes to important matters. I never wanted a job that paid a commission—I am a salary kind of girl.

Gordon feels sorry for people like me. He loves the excitement and thrill of creating opportunities and making things happen and having no boundaries. He delights in setting goals and achieving them. He once made me listen to a Tony Robbins instructional series on goal setting with him. Every morning before work we spent 30 minutes listening to the tapes and completing each exercise assigned on the tape.

It took us six months to complete the series, but the result was a set of specific, written goals with timeframes. For years, every New Year's Day Gordon pulled out those pages and reviewed them with me, making sure we were on track.

He didn't feel stressed when big deals were won or lost or when big things were happening at the office. He would come home from work, tell me about the intense thing going on, and I would be the one lying awake all night, worrying. He slept like a baby, knowing I was doing the worrying for him.

Only once did I see real fear on Gordon's face. We were living in a dumpy apartment in the East Bay. I came home from work and was shocked to see Gordon sitting at the kitchen table. He never came home before 7pm but not today. He was talking on the telephone, leaving an urgent message for someone to call him back. I waited for him to finish the call then waited for him to explain the terrible look on his face.

Gordon told me that the payroll taxes at his company had not been paid in months. His partner, David, ran the administrative side of the business which included paying the bills and Gordon ran sales and was responsible for all revenue. As with most early-stage companies, money was extremely tight. David paid the bills that absolutely had to be paid to keep the doors open—the telephone bill, employee salaries, utilities, and rent. For a stretch of time there wasn't enough money to pay all the bills so he shorted the IRS.

David planned to pay the IRS as soon as there was money enough to cover the shortfall. He hadn't told Gordon because he fully expected to resolve the issue before it became anything to worry about. It didn't work out that way. Instead, the IRS contacted David that day and told him that he and Gordon were going to jail if they didn't pay $20,000 in 24 hours. So Gordon was home calling anyone he knew, trying to raise his half of this debt and David was at his home, doing the same thing.

The irony is that in my years of working, paying my debts, and saving for the future, I had saved a total of $10,000, the exact amount Gordon needed this very day. Gordon had no idea I had the money.

Moments like this give a person the opportunity to ask herself, "Who am I really?" As a Christian, I know the pitfalls of loving money too much. I am guilty in this department. I easily fall into the mindset of "I am a good and generous person, but don't ask me for my hard-earned cash." I will happily donate items I no longer want, just don't expect me to write a check.

In the story of Cain and Abel, Abel gave to God his first fruits, the best he had to offer. In contrast Cain gave to God what he didn't need, what was left over. Cain hated his brother for his obedience to God because it reflected Cain's greed like a mirror reflecting an ugly image of himself. Rather than acknowledge his own guilt in the mirror of his brother's devotion and repent, Cain killed Abel.

In scripture, we are reminded that everything we have is a gift from God, from the first fruits to the leftovers. All that we have—our health, our loved ones, our belongings, our abilities, even our lives—can disappear in a moment. The act of giving reminds us to be grateful and to acknowledge that God first gave to us the gifts that made our good fortunes possible. Giving is a beautiful way of saying thank you.

As a Christian, I am called to give to those in need with no expectation of repayment. That is a tough one for this cheap Mid-Western farm girl. Jesus summed up the Law in two commandments: Love God above all and love your neighbor as yourself. Was God first in my life or was the almighty dollar? And, how would I want to be treated?

My natural inclination is be Cain and give what is left over or justify not giving at all by saying I worked hard for that money, it's mine, and I am keeping it. With Gordon's situation, God was calling me to be Abel and give the best of what I had. He was calling me to give *all* that I had.

So what was I going to do? Would I keep my mouth shut and let Gordon keep on trying to frantically borrow from friends, or was I going to speak up and end his suffering right now?

Not one person picked up the phone when Gordon called to ask for a loan. In the time it took for him to leave a "Please call me. It is urgent" message on another answering machine, I had come to terms with what was going to happen next. I was going to give him the money and I would never see that money again.

Gordon was dumbfounded when I told him I had $10,000 and that it was his to pay his debt. He promised he would never stop working to make a success of himself and his company and that he would pay me back, no matter how long it took.

I believed he would work hard, but I did not think I would ever be repaid. It didn't matter. I had already said goodbye to the money.

He and his partner paid the IRS and the threat of jail was gone. True to his word, Gordon brought me a $200 check every month. Four years and two months later, the debt was paid in full.

12

We Almost Made It

With both of us working, we eventually bought a house, had our two children, and started to breathe a little easier in our financial situation. Then again, I yearned to be home and raise my own children. At the same time, Gordon yearned to be done with the business he worked so hard to build. It had been 15 years of heavy responsibility, terrible hours and big risk. He was tired.

Gordon and his partners were all ready to move on so there were no objections when a buyer came knocking on the door. The buyer was an up and coming international sales company who planned to retain Gordon's employees—all 150 of them. Gordon and his partners would be paid in stock and Gordon would join the sales team at the parent company as an employee.

For the first time in 15 years, Gordon was going to receive a regular paycheck, work normal hours, and get a paid vacation. It was 1999, a time when people were making millions of dollars in stock deals and the purchasing company was poised to go *big*.

All the pieces were falling into place, ready to reward us for the years of hard work and sacrifice. Things seemed to be going our way and we appreciated it.

I was beside myself with happiness and so was Gordon. The two companies seemed like a perfect fit. So the deal was done. Gordon would continue to sell for the new company and in a few years, our stock would pay off big and our dreams of prosperity would come true.

Alas, plans go awry. The overwhelming mismanagement of the purchasing company's new leadership team soon put all our plans in a death spiral. Against all Gordon's warnings and pleas for thoughtful action, the company made disastrous business decisions and quickly marched toward bankruptcy.

I tell this story only because of what happened next.

Word came out that all Gordon's former employees, all 150 of them, were being laid off. The company was sending someone from HR to give them the news that afternoon.

Gordon would not allow that to happen. He had hired most of those people. He knew them personally and he knew their families. He and his partners had sold the company under the promise that these people would be treated well and that they would be able to continue their careers. There was no way Gordon would allow a stranger from HR to tell them their hard earned skills were no longer needed.

Many of his employees had been considered unemployable for anything but minimum wage jobs when they showed up at his door. Many had no high school diploma, few had attended college, some had prison records, one was actively serving time but was allowed to work during the day and return to prison in the evenings. The company was a melting pot of race, religion, experience, and ability.

Gordon was more interested in an applicant's character. Reliable? Strong work ethic? Interested in learning? Work well with a team while meeting individual goals? If the answer to these questions was yes, he gave the person a chance.

For those that made the cut, it was a chance to work hard and have a career, not just a job. It was a chance to gain marketable skills and experience and create a future full of opportunity for themselves.

This melting pot was full of people who cared for each other. Now they were going to be told the pot was being emptied. Gordon wanted to be the person to tell them. He explained what was going on at the parent company and how it was affecting this team. He apologized for this terrible turn of events and assured them that he was losing his job too. He offered to be a reference for anyone applying for a new position. He thanked them for their hard work and for their part in making the company into a place where people were successful, loved their jobs, and made lifelong friends.

When Gordon was done speaking, a line of people began to form. One by one, his former employees shook Gordon's hand and thanked him. They thanked him for respecting them enough to show up in person and give them the news. They thanked him for believing in their potential when they came looking for work and for giving them the opportunity to set a new course for their lives. Some told stories of their "pre-company" days, their lack of direction, and often wayward ways. All expressed sadness at having to leave this place and these people who had become like family to them.

Not once did Gordon lament the loss of his stock value. He didn't lament the loss of his first job with a regular paycheck. In true Gordon fashion, he turned toward the future and contemplated what he would do next.

13

It Is Time to Leave

With no convincing or coercing, we both came to the same conclusion: we wanted to leave California and start anew. Where did we want to go? We pulled out our kids' kitchen placemat with the U.S. map on it and lay it on the table. For no particular reason, we both focused on Portland, Oregon.

Neither of us had been there. We knew nothing about it. Some friends had moved there a few months before, but that was about all we knew. We considered the East Coast, but quickly decided against that. Something about Portland called to us, but how would we make all this happen?

The Good Lord moves in mysterious ways. A week after our contemplation with the placemat, Gordon got a telephone call from a corporate recruiter. The recruiter was looking to place a Vice President of Sales in a Fortune 500 company located in Vancouver, Washington, just across the Columbia River from Portland, Oregon.

This was the moment we were hoping for. This was going to be the culmination of all our hard work and sacrifice. Gordon was hired into a prestigious and stable position, he was earning a good salary and, as he wanted, he had huge potential earning power depending on the performance of his sales team.

It was as if we were being propelled to this moment. From the day we looked at the map to the day we got the job offer to the day I quit my job and sold our house in California to the day we moved into our new home in Lake Oswego to the day Gordon started his new job, only 5 weeks had passed. The speed and miraculous coordination of all the events that made these changes possible were breathtaking.

We were so happy and felt so blessed. Things seemed to be going our way and we appreciated it.

As Gordon settled into his new position, he soon saw that something was terribly wrong. His new company had represented growth and opportunity during the interview process. The reality was layoffs, shrinking profits and a sales organization that was in total disarray. One month into the job, Gordon laid off half the sales force. Three months into the job, Gordon recognized the symptoms of a corporate death spiral. In six months the company filed for bankruptcy and Gordon was again out of a job.

Now what? It was August 2001 and we were in a new town where we knew no one. Gordon didn't have an excellent sales reputation here as he did in the Bay Area. He had no reputation at all. With his usual determination and discipline, Gordon wasted no time lamenting what had happened. He went into his home office, shut the door, and started making telephone calls, looking for job opportunities.

Within a few days he was lining up interviews. We stayed calm and hopeful. This was certainly a bump in our road but we remained cautiously optimistic. Gordon would land a new job and we would resume our plans of "happily ever after," it was just going to be with a different company.

But this vision of "happily ever after" was not to be. Three weeks after Gordon lost his job, 9-11 happened. The United States was attacked by Islamic terrorists and thousands of innocent people were killed. The entire country went into mourning. The bottom fell out of the job market. All Gordon's interviews were cancelled. There were no jobs to be had. We had no contacts, no income, and no prospects for future prosperity. This was very, very bad.

Gordon was done allowing others to determine his professional fate. From now on, things were going to be different. He loved sales and wanted to stay in sales, but he would no longer look for permanent employment. As a sales consultant, he could affect positive change in other sales teams then leave. There would be no staff meetings, no time wasting, no employer/employee issues, no company politics, just action that brought measurable results. He could hire and train people, establish sales processes, and implement strategies to keep teams on track. When his work was done, he would move on to the next client. This was an environment where all Gordon's skills could shine.

The long slog of starting a sales consulting practice began. The only person Gordon had met in our short time in Portland was the pastor at our church. Even though he didn't really know us, the pastor hesitantly gave Gordon a couple names of people in the congregation to call. One by one, Gordon started calling people, setting meetings, asking for referrals, and expanding his network of professional contacts.

It took two long years to get the practice going. For two long years, Gordon worked to earn consulting contracts and build a reputation. For two long years, I did everything I could to not make any unnecessary expenditure, maintain a positive attitude, and not let Gordon or the kids see how hard this was on me. I was welcome to cry in the closet but when I walked out, I needed to face our challenges with a "can do" attitude. If I crumbled under the pressure of such economic uncertainty, the whole endeavor was going to crumble with me. I could not let that happen.

I didn't understand. Why did we have to start over again? What were we missing? We were honest, ethical people. We were hard-working people, willing to put in the time and effort to build our success. We weren't looking for lucky breaks or shortcuts. Yet every time we got close to comfort and prosperity, everything we built was knocked down in front of us. It was painful.

Every day I prayed that God would help us through this dark time. I felt helpless because for the first time, I didn't have a job to help with the bills. There was no income. Period. I had been so sure our move to Oregon was God-ordained. And now this? What lesson were we to learn? Did the learning process really need to hurt so much?

Slowly, Gordon gained momentum and his sales consulting practice began to thrive. Slowly, we paid ourselves back the money we spent during the startup years. Slowly, we began to build the life we envisioned when we moved to Oregon.

By 2007, Gordon was hitting all his business and income goals. He had an excellent reputation in the business community. We had wonderful friends. We were regular volunteers at the kids' schools and around town. After so much time and work and anguish and success, things were going our way and we appreciated it.

Then in March 2008 Gordon suffered a massive stroke.

All the pieces of my life took on different significance as I began to comprehend the consequences of this life-changing event. Gordon and I had certainly experienced our share of struggles and loss as well as success and achievement. We had learned to persevere through the bad times and appreciate the good times. The challenges made us tougher and more resilient. Yet more importantly, joy came easily to us. It didn't take much to make us happy.

All those life experiences, challenges, setbacks, successes, and decisions that molded and shaped me were coming together for this moment. All this time, God was preparing me, building my character, and teaching me to rely on Him, not my own ability or on the stuff around me. He wrestled with me, pinning me in a few short moves until I could only look up and acknowledge that He had the power. He was the One with the strength and who promised to support me as I carried this load.

Since we were starting a new life, Gordon and I decided to read Rick Warren's book, *The Purpose Driven Life*, together to get some ideas. The first words were "It's not about you." Brother, did I know that.

14

Recovery

Stroke recovery is either a mystery or a closely guarded secret. I began to accept that there was no roadmap for us to follow. Pretty much all the literature we received was about recognizing stroke and preventing stroke—not particularly helpful for us at this juncture. As for what to do after a massive stroke? We had to chart our own course. And as the advertisement in the hospital waiting room said, "Time is Brain." Thanks for reminding me.

We had to plan, and quickly. The general guideline we heard most was "If you don't have it back in two years, you probably won't get it back." We had 20 therapy sessions available to us through the end of that year, according to our health insurance plan. After that, our deductible would start over and we couldn't afford all that out-of-pocket expense. I carefully scheduled all of them. We couldn't afford to go over our number and there was no way I was going to leave an appointment unused.

I scheduled 17 Occupational Therapy sessions so Gordon could focus on getting his upper body working. I scheduled 3 Physical Therapy sessions to help his walking. Once we had directions, I figured we could do the rest. There was no room for Speech Therapy; we were going to have to figure that out on our own.

At every therapy session, I studied the exercises the therapists did with Gordon. I drew pictures and wrote descriptions in a notebook so I could replicate them at home. I became a master of the stick figure, drawing all the positions and motions Gordon and I would work on together.

As we got more and more exercises to work on, I redrew all my pictures and typed my notes onto recipe cards and filed them in a box labeled Gordon's Exercise Box. I color-coded them by the tools we used and filed them by body part being exercised. Over time, we accumulated too many exercises to do in a day so I created a monthly calendar, providing us with a little variety. We could not allow ourselves to become bored or complacent. We needed to keep our momentum and motivation to see improvement.

We had to get Gordon out of the wheelchair and walking again. Taking walks together had always been a big part of our relationship. From the first day we met, through all the lean years when we couldn't afford any other entertainment, to now living in Oregon with all its beautiful scenery, Gordon and I walked together. We talked, laughed, planned, celebrated, reflected—all while walking. When our kids were little, we bought a double stroller so they could come with us.

At Christmas time, Gordon decorated the stroller with battery operated lights and dangled decorations from the canopy. He stuck a boom box in the lower basket so we could listen to Christmas carols while we walked. We bundled up the kids and walked through neighborhoods, looking at Christmas lights. We bought a double jogging stroller so we could bring the kids rollerblading with us in the summer. It was time for all of us to be together with no distractions. It was exercise, fresh air, communication and fun all wrapped up in a no-cost package.

To walk again, Gordon was first going to have to find his right leg. Sounds strange, doesn't it? He was so disconnected from his right side that he didn't really know where it was.

The muscles in his hip that held his leg in place weren't responding, causing his whole leg to be rotated out. Instead of both feet facing forward when he stood, his right foot pointed out to the right, perpendicular to his left foot, like half a ballet dancer.

He couldn't lift the front of his foot to take a step so he had a brace that kept his foot at a right angle to his leg. Rather than lift his knee when he took a step, Gordon would tilt his hip and throw his leg out and around. He had no idea he wasn't walking correctly. All the mechanics of walking had to be relearned and practiced.

One comment from a therapist continued to haunt me through that first year: "You never know when he will stop improving. This may be all you get."

In addition to all the physical changes, Gordon was also going through wild behavioral changes. Like a child going through his "terrible two's," Gordon's damaged brain was bringing on a series of childlike phases, each lasting several weeks before entering a new childlike phase. As each phase began, I fought the memory of that therapist's comment. What if his improvement stops here? What if he remains like this, in this phase, from now on?

The first and longest-lasting phase was his lack of filter when it came to expressing his thoughts. You know how little kids say exactly what they think when they think it? So did Gordon. When we first brought him home from the hospital, Rachel and I rolled him in his wheelchair outside as much as the weather would allow. Rachel would stick an oversized badminton racket in his good hand and hit birdies to him, trying to get him to hit it back. Our neighbor boy, Will, who was 12 at the time and going through a growth spurt, politely walked across the driveway to say hello. Gordon looked at him and blurted, like a five year old, "You used to be chubby." Blushing bright red, Will turned around and walked back to his house. Gordon looked at me incredulously. "Why did I say that?" he asked.

I made great effort to cook Gordon's favorite foods now that he was home. Even Rachel and Tom were excited about dinner those first few weeks. Yet after each meal, Gordon would look at me with a disapproving face and say, "That wasn't very good."

Not very good? Even the kids liked dinner and they complain about something at *every* meal!

Gordon couldn't be specific about what was wrong, he just screwed up his face and shook his head. I knew he wasn't in his right mind, but what does that have to do with food? I was more puzzled than insulted. After about three months, Gordon noticed that he was beginning to get feeling back in the right side of his face and that food tasted better. It turned out that my cooking wasn't the problem; the taste buds on the right side of his mouth hadn't been working.

Along with that lack of filter came cursing. Neither Gordon nor I are fans of vulgar language. We do not curse and generally try to keep our words at a higher standard. For a while, Gordon had a profound lapse in that standard.

We still laugh about the Jeopardy incident. Our favorite television show is Jeopardy. We record it the night before and watch every day, testing ourselves on our knowledge of whatever they may be featuring. We were such fans of the show that Rachel's first song as a toddler was the Jeopardy Theme song.

Pre-stroke, whenever someone would get the Daily Double, Gordon would always call out, "Bet it all!" When the cursing phase was in full swing, Gordon, as usual, called out, "Bet it all!" One episode, when the contestant did not bet it all, he declared loudly, "What a dick!" Everyone but Gordon froze. Slowly, Rachel and Tommy turned and looked at me, eyes big as saucers. Never, ever, had they heard their father say such a thing. I calmly told Gordon that what he said was unnecessary and that he should be more careful with his words. He had no idea he had said something inappropriate.

Then there was the lying phase. Just like a child, Gordon would tell little lies, just to see if he could get away with it.

- "Did you brush your teeth?"

  "Yes." (Clearly, he had not.)

- "Did you drink your juice?"

  "Yes." (He had not. His full glass of juice was still on the table.)

- "Did you take your pill?"

  "Yes." (He had not. His pill was still lying next to his full glass of juice.)

- "Did you get out of that chair without anyone nearby to keep you from falling?"

  "No." (He was standing alone in the middle of the room. Clearly, he had.)

It was so annoying! I already had two children who were long past this phase! Now I essentially had a third child. He was a husband, father, and child—all at the same time. All those parts of him needed to be cared for in their own way.

Then there was stubborn Gordon. Gordon was on a blood thinner for the first six months after his stroke while his carotid arteries healed. It was very important that he *not* fall. If he fell, not only would he probably injure himself and have more to recover from, but there was also a chance that he would bleed internally. Falling would be *very* bad. I stressed this truth to him regularly, especially when he didn't want to wait for me to help him in and out of the wheelchair or up and down the stairs. In true childlike fashion, he would say, "I can do it myself!"

One evening, I was making dinner and Gordon was sitting at the kitchen table, working on math sheets. I was only four feet away from him. Suddenly, Gordon went crashing onto the floor. I dropped everything and knelt beside him, trying to assess his condition and figure out what happened. As he lay on the floor, I could see that he wasn't bleeding externally. We checked function on both sides of his body. All seemed undamaged.

As he lay there, gathering his recollection of what had just happened, Gordon looked at me with frightened eyes. I tried to ask calmly what happened. He had decided to get up out of the chair, but he had forgotten that his right side didn't work. He had pivoted to the right and tried to stand, but ended up on the floor instead. Again, I tried to calmly remind him that I needed to help him stand up and that falling was bad. With the shamed look of a child caught in the act, he said, "Now I will believe you."

Oh, did I want to scold him. I wanted to treat him like the petulant child he was. He deserved an angry talking-to, a time out, a punishment. He was disregarding all my warnings and cautions. Every time he behaved badly, I paid the price. If he hurt himself further, I would be the one picking up the pieces, taking on more responsibility for his recovery.

"You never know when he will stop improving. This may be all you get."

Oh dear God, I cried in the closet during Gordon's nap time, *please don't let it end here. Please get him—us—through this. I still need to see only one set of footprints in the sand because I cannot carry this load.*

Husband. Father. Head of household. Respect. Cherish. Unconditional love. Till death do us part. While death sounded pretty good, I couldn't leave Gordon...or the kids. I could not say or do all those angry things that hung in the back of my mind, teasing me with how good it would feel to let them fly out. I had to be the grownup. *I give it all to you, Jesus. I am so weak.*

Then there was the Gory Movie phase. This one scared me. I don't know what happens in a man's brain that makes him like gory movies, but whatever it is, it hit Gordon like a drug. I don't even know how it got started.

One evening, I found Gordon watching the movie, "Saw," on television. He was entranced. Within days, we started getting deliveries of all the Saw and Hostel movies in the mail. He couldn't seem to get enough of the violence, blood, torture, and death in those horrible movies. He was mesmerized by the screaming, begging, and crying. When I saw the DVDs arriving in the mail, I immediately changed the request list on the DVD delivery website. I went through the list of recorded shows on our DVR and deleted all the crazy violent movies he was hoping to watch.

What in the world was going on in his head? What part of his brain was being stimulated to the point of addiction with the excessive violence and horror in these films? His brain was so vulnerable, and he was filling it with awful things! What would be the effect of this? What was he becoming? Would this affect his behavior in the long-term?

It had to stop. I waited for a calm moment to talk to Gordon. He didn't know why he liked the movies so much. He couldn't tell me anything specific about how the movies made him feel. He just knew he wanted to watch them. I explained to him that these movies were not okay. His brain was working hard to recover and rewire, and this kind of input could not lead to anything good. We needed to focus on more positive input.

It was a good moment for us. Gordon was completely reasonable and said he understood my concerns. He agreed to stop recording horror flicks, but I continued to monitor his viewing, just in case we were still in the lying phase.

I mentioned that the first and longest-lasting phase was his lack of filter when it came to expressing his thoughts, saying exactly what he thought when he thought it. That lack of filter also applied to his emotions.

Gordon was helpless in containing or controlling his emotional behavior. On one end of the spectrum, he would tell me 20-30 times a day how much he loved me. On the other end, he would explode in anger over any little thing. It was shocking, frightening, and unpredictable, especially to Rachel and Tom.

84

15

The Children

How does a child make sense of all this?

Gordon had always been their healthy, active dad: playing with them, running around on the beach, tossing them in the pool, walking on his hands to amaze their friends, a fun guy! Now, he was completely different.

Our son, Tom, was only 12 years old, just a 7th grader, when it happened. He didn't act out and start getting into trouble or anything like that. He didn't let his grades slip or even visit the counselor at school, although she tried to talk to him once or twice. He kept it all inside. Thankfully, he and I have a very close relationship and we still made time to watch cartoons and laugh together.

Then again, Tom stayed away from Gordon. I couldn't blame him. His dad didn't look the same or sound the same, and he responded erratically in otherwise normal situations. It was scary and unpredictable—two things to which Tom does not respond well. Gordon was no longer the father he knew.

Gordon's emotional instability was frightening. Because his perception of time was messed up, he couldn't always tell how long it had been between his request and another's response.

One evening, Gordon was sitting at the table and Tom was watching television. Gordon said, "Tommy, bring me my cane." Before Tommy had a chance to even get up out of the chair, Gordon, thinking he was being ignored and that plenty of time had passed for Tommy to comply, screamed, "Get my cane!"

We were never the yelling kind of parents. These angry outbursts were totally uncharacteristic of Gordon and only made him more frightening and unrecognizable to the kids.

Tom retreated from Gordon as much as he could yet still live in the same house. Tom has always been a sensitive soul and has never responded well to yelling. While he was growing up, I never really had to discipline him or punish him. All I had to say was "Tommy, I am disappointed in you." He would be so disappointed in himself and so apologetic that I didn't need to pile on. With his dad now so unpredictable, Tom stayed clear. The trust between them was broken.

Rachel, Daddy's little girl, was a little tougher. She was also a little older than Tommy, so that perhaps gave her more understanding. It was very upsetting for her to experience her dad's volatility, but she hung in there with him. Rather than avoid him, she was more cautious around him, ready to run if things got loud.

Rachel was 14 and a 9th grader. Her perspective was more about herself than about Gordon, and she was just angry. Why couldn't things go her way? She was looking forward to someday driving Gordon's BMW...but I sold the car while he was in the hospital. She was looking forward to our vacation ...*canceled*. Her 15th birthday was a week after Gordon came home from the hospital, so planning a party was out of the question. She didn't want Gordon to go *anywhere* with her because she didn't want people looking at us, wondering, *What's wrong with that guy?*

She wanted her life to be normal. She wanted vacations, dinners out, shopping trips, opportunities to do things and go places. She wanted what a lot of girls in our town had and took for granted. She did not want to be different. She did not want her dad to be different.

All household activity now revolved around Gordon and his needs. The kids were no longer the central focus of my day and that was hard for all of us. They were used to having me take care of all the chores around the house as well as be available to them whenever they needed me. Now they had to pitch in and help. Not that kids helping with chores is a bad thing, but for us, each chore was a reminder of what had happened, what we had lost, and how our lives had changed.

Every now and then, Rachel and Tom would mention something happening at school or with their friends. I heard the wisdom and pain of experience in their voices as they recounted the event and gave me their perspective. In pre-stroke days, they each would have been all worked up over what was happening. Now, they were usually irked at the silliness of the drama. How dare someone be so upset over a little thing while my kids were dealing with true sorrow?

We did what we could to make home as normal as possible. I still got up every morning and made their breakfasts before school. I still tucked them into bed every night and said prayers with them by their beds. We kept our Saturday morning routine of going to the bagel restaurant.

When the kids complained about the changes in our lives, I tried to calmly turn the conversation to needing them to be part of the team and to the importance of all of us working together. There was no blaming Dad for any of this. He was an innocent victim, just like we were. I sincerely needed their cooperation. There was no way I could handle everything by myself.

Even today, my kids don't like to talk about what happened. Instead, they have great fun pointing out all the things Gordon still does wrong because of the stroke, and Gordon is an amazingly good sport about it.

Tom does a great impersonation of Gordon, in those early days of therapy, trying to lift his elbows out to his side. He takes big, deep breaths, puffs his cheeks out, and throws his elbows up, like the Hulk in reverse. Then he drops his arms and breathes loudly from feigned exhaustion. It is a spot-on impersonation. Yet underneath, I think they laugh and tease as a way to deal with the hurt, fear, and frustration.

When people ask me how the stroke has affected Rachel and Tom, I always say that I will know in 20 years. However, there are telltale signs now of the stroke's effects. Those signs can be summed up in two words: stability and predictability.

Both Rachel and Tom started little businesses when they were youngsters. They both had that entrepreneurial spirit and were motivated to earn their own money by providing a service. Rachel sold snow cones and did lots of babysitting. Tom was a pet-sitter and watered people's plants when they were on vacation. They both created and circulated flyers to advertise their business ventures. They both made money and were proud of their accomplishments.

Within a year or two of the stroke, Tom started talking about joining the Army. I am guessing that the Army's structure and predictability is appealing to him after all that happened to us. Rachel's ambitions have fluctuated between the desire to help people and the desire to make lots of money. Predictability appeals to her as well. She has made it perfectly clear that she only wants to work for large companies where processes, procedures, and financial statements are dependable and stable.

We haven't seen it yet, but I hope a long-term effect is appreciation and admiration for their father and his amazing optimism and tenacity.

One day, maybe when they have families of their own, both Rachel and Tom will talk about our family and how we went through such difficult times, but that we made the best of it.

I hope they recognize and appreciate the strength of our marriage and our commitment to our marriage vows. I hope they choose their own spouses wisely.

Most of all, I hope they thank the Good Lord for holding us close to Him, never abandoning us and never leaving us to drift alone.

16

Back to Recovery

When Gordon acted up, I absolutely could not get
angry or yell back. I had to be calm, diplomatic, consistent,
and parental. Just like a mother, I firmly told him he was not
allowed to talk like that. He needed to use kind words and
speak respectfully. He needed to give Tommy time to get up
and retrieve the cane.

Gordon struggled to comprehend what he had done and soon
realized he had been out of line. Like a child, he dropped his
head and looked at his feet. With a sad face and pleading
voice, he looked up at me, apologizing and begging me to
forgive him.

Each time one of these outbursts occurred, he would agonize
over what he had done and continue to ask for forgiveness,
even though I had told him it was okay and that I was not
angry. He apologized to Rachel and Tommy, but they knew it
likely would happen again and remained on their guard.

It was evident that Gordon was not in his right mind. He was
saying and doing things he *never* would do before his terrible
brain injury. He tried to get better but the erratic behavior
was out of his control. I knew all these things, and yet—
once—he still hurt my feelings. Even worse, he did it on
purpose.

I had again told him that he could not stand up without someone there to help him if he needed help. We could not risk him falling. Gordon began to argue with me, claiming he could stand up just fine and did not need help. I firmly said it was not okay and that he needed to wait for me.

Gordon looked at me indignantly, and declared in biting, kindergarten style, "I don't love you anymore," and turned his face away from me. I knew he didn't mean it. I knew he was just trying to hurt my feelings and, doggone it, he was successful. Isn't that silly? It was like a stab in my heart to hear those words.

For all the wild, erratic behavior Gordon displayed, he also displayed completely normal behavior. The perpetual roller coaster ride of recovery combined the ups and downs of unrecognizable conduct with the straight-aways of the old Gordon we all knew and loved.

Yet like a roller coaster in the dark, the rider doesn't know when the twists and turns are coming. Not being a thrill ride lover myself, I just wanted it to end. Slowly but surely, Gordon moved through the phases of this second childhood, gradually displaying more normal, adult behavior for longer periods of time. Dips and curves appeared less dramatically and less often as time went on, but I needed to be prepared, just in case.

It still makes me smile when I remember how concerned Gordon was that he would never be funny again. Pre-stroke, he was very quick-witted and clever. Together, we laughed a lot and we joked with Rachel and Tommy. When Rachel was a preschooler moving out of the literal stage, Gordon would say something goofy and she would ask, very seriously, "Was that a joke?" When Gordon said yes, she would break into peals of laughter—she didn't want to get it wrong!

Post-stroke, Gordon still wanted to be funny. He thought funny thoughts and he laughed at funny things around him. He just couldn't speak funny things. The possibility of not being funny was one of the few things that could bring down Gordon's mood. At first, he tried to say something to make me laugh and it didn't make any sense at all. Later, he tried and instead said things that were completely insulting. I assured him that humor would return, but basic language had to come first.

One evening, Gordon was telling me how he had tried to make a joke but it didn't come out right and there was no laughter. He elaborated by telling me that in the silence, he could almost hear the "chipmunks." When I finally stopped laughing, I told him, "You meant crickets—you could almost hear the crickets!" The chipmunk comment became my recurring punch line around the house for weeks.

Without humor, I believe we would be in a very different place right now. If our only reactions to our challenges were anger and frustration, I would probably be depressed and alone. Laughter reunited us as a family.

At first, Rachel and Tommy didn't laugh at Gordon's crazy behavior because they didn't know how he would react. As his personality slowly became more recognizable and they got used to his speech and physical difficulties, we were able to find humor in his changes.

Gordon quickly learned that the more he could laugh at himself, the more approachable he became. The sillier his mistake, the more we would laugh. It took time, but the mood in the house slowly returned to Happy. The way Gordon interacts with our kids now is almost normal. "Almost normal" is a beautiful blessing.

17

Our New Normal Begins to Form

Gordon's stroke changed everything in our lives. I think of those science fiction shows where some mysterious thing happens and, although everything looks the same, nothing actually is the same, like "Invasion of the Body Snatchers."

Our house looked the same. Our neighborhood looked the same. I drove the same car. We wore our same clothes. Yet, everything was different.

The structure of our day was different. What we could and could not do was different. Pre-stroke, my typical day was getting the kids off to school, walking with my friends, working around the house, pulling some weeds, and volunteering for my favorite organizations. Gordon's typical day was going to appointments, working with clients, cold calling, reading, and planning for the next day.

For the first couple of years post-stroke, I got the kids off to school and spent the rest of the day entirely focused on Gordon and his recovery. He had good days and bad days. He had days in which he was awake and alert, and he had days in which he was exhausted and couldn't pull together his thoughts or words.

Every day was focused on his exercises and the possibility of even a tiny improvement in his mind and body.

Whenever we were outside and ran into people we knew from our pre-stroke days, I found myself hoping and wishing they would say, "Wow! Gordon is getting so much better!" or "I can hardly tell anything happened!" Yet no one ever said these things.

Instead, they commented kindly on how well Gordon was walking or on how far we were walking. Every kind word was appreciated, but the sadness of it all quietly stayed with me. I just couldn't let it show.

For a break, every afternoon during those first few months I would help Gordon into the car and drive him around town. He looked out the window and took in the view, as if he were seeing our neighborhood for the first time.

We slowly drove past friends' houses and I told him who lived there and how we knew them. I wanted him to say "I remember them!" or "I remember that place!" but he didn't. He just gazed at the scenery.

18

Who Am I Now?

In the quiet moments, looking around at this house that looked the same but wasn't the same, I had time to think.

I thought about our marriage vows and about the blessing the pastor prayed over us. I thought about how much we loved living here and how we had been so blessed with good things.

I thought about how hard we had worked all these years, always in lock-step with our goals and our plans to achieve them. I thought about our current financial circumstances and wondered what in the world was going to happen to us.

I thought about my priorities, now that everything had changed.

It was a time when I began to understand what Saint Paul meant about love when he wrote 1 Corinthians 13 (NLT).

> *If I speak in the tongues of men or of angels, but do not have love, I am only a resounding gong or a clanging cymbal. If I have the gift of prophecy and can fathom all mysteries and all knowledge, and if I have a faith that can move mountains, but do not have love, I am nothing. If I give all I possess to the poor and give over my body to hardship that I may boast, but do not have love, I gain nothing.*

Love is patient, love is kind. It does not envy, it does not boast, it is not proud. It does not dishonor others, it is not self-seeking, it is not easily angered, it keeps no record of wrongs. Love does not delight in evil but rejoices with the truth. It always protects, always trusts, always hopes, always perseveres. Love never fails...

And now these three remain: faith, hope and love. But the greatest of these is love.

I had never thought of that section of scripture as a roadmap for my day-to-day life, but now it was. I was going to love Gordon no matter what he looked or sounded like. He was still my husband and I was going to treat him as such, even though he was going through wild changes.

If I treated Gordon like a child, I would soon think of him as a child and our relationship would not return to what it had been. What's more, if I let anger and disappointment creep into our relationship, we would not return to who we had been. I was going to be Gordon's wife and I was going to protect, trust, hope, and persevere, just like Saint Paul wrote.

I was going to be happy for people who were experiencing good things. I was not going to be resentful of those who were prospering. I was going to be honest about our situation with no judgment of those who insinuated that perhaps we had done something to deserve this. I was not going to seek pity or expect people to keep attending to us. They were going to get on with their lives and we were going to get on with ours.

I was not going to harbor ill feelings toward the ER doctor who sent us home in the early stages of the stroke—he did his best. Instead, I was going to be thankful for all of Gordon's improvements and be fully aware that all recovery is a gift from Almighty God.

Jesus lived among us for thirty-something years. He had friends and family, challenges and struggles, laughter and tears. He lived the human experience and showed us how to do it correctly. He showed us the nature of God, the love of God. He showed compassion for every person, regardless of their sinfulness. He allowed Himself to be tortured and crucified as the ultimate sacrifice and payment for all our sins. On the morning of His resurrection, His first words were about peace and compassion.

He has compassion for me too. Who better to admit my powerlessness to than the One with all the power Who truly loves me? I have always known Jesus as my Lord and Savior, the One who forgives my sins and who will welcome me to Heaven when my time on this earth is over. Surrendering my life, worries, and challenges to Jesus was the only option and, ultimately, a huge relief. I have no fight left in me, and I am learning to be okay with that.

Every day, I remember my position—a servant with a servant's heart—and make the effort to shed the expectations and desires of this world. It's hard. We live in this world and it is quite natural to want worldly things. And I don't think that wanting worldly things is wrong, either. What is wrong is making those worldly things more important than they should be.

By putting worldly things out of our reach, we had the opportunity to realign our thinking and our priorities. I think of it as the painful blessing of putting God first in my life.

19

Acceptance

Part of my New Normal is no longer thinking about retirement, or even thinking much about the future at all. What is the point of thinking about it? I am going to get through this week, and that is about it. It seems that the moment I start to plan and create a sense of control, everything goes sideways. I am reminded again and again that I am not in control. It isn't about me.

Another part of my New Normal is accepting that my friendships have changed. I used to have an active social life and a wonderful network of friends. Although I still consider those women to be my friends, I am now disconnected from all the activities and socializing. This is no one's fault and I accept that there was no choice in this. My life went off the rails, not theirs. However, the process of disconnecting has been painful.

I missed my friends at the beginning of recovery and I still miss them today. I hear about their trips and parties and events together and I feel that pain of loss because I am no longer part of it and likely never will be again. I don't have much to say when we run into each other at the grocery store other than "I am fine" and "Gordon is doing better." I make the effort to be happy for them and I am happy to see them, but honestly, it is bittersweet.

I have a few beautiful women who still are my "go to" girls. We put in the effort to keep our friendships strong. We make time to talk, laugh, and encourage each other. We may not see each other often, but we certainly make the most of our time together. A phone call, a text, a quick cup of coffee, all help me feel connected and blessed to have these women in my life.

Occasionally, the dream of the bus running me over still enters my mind. I have to admit, there are times when that still sounds pretty good. There are times when I am tired of the struggle. I have always been an optimist—a glass half full kind of girl. Now I struggle for my optimism. I want to be hopeful but the little voice in my head warns me that all our progress could come crashing down again. I am like a dog that has been kicked too many times. I am hunkered down, protecting myself. It is hard to be open and excited when one has learned to always be on guard.

This bothers me. I don't want to be anything other than optimistic. I am reminded of a story of a fisherman who only kept the little fish he caught and threw the big ones back into the water. When asked why, he replied, "I only have a ten-inch frying pan." I don't want to live with the limitations of a ten-inch frying pan. I want to be open to receive abundant life, whatever that might look like. I don't want to be so guarded against the ups and the downs that I can't experience the joy I know God has for me.

I certainly don't want to pass my struggle on to my kids. There are joy, love, happiness and blessings to be had out there in the world and I want Rachel and Tom to experience them. I want them to know that no matter how wonderful or how difficult life is, God holds them in the palm of His hand and that He loves them with the love of a perfect father. Of this they can rest assured.

How I carry myself in this phase of my life matters. How I live each day is a choice. I choose to look heavenward and ask, "What do You have for me today?"

In my journey of surrender, I promise to accept what comes and to willingly go where He leads me.

> *God is our refuge and strength, an ever-present help in trouble (Psalm 46:1 NIV).*

20

Becoming New Gordon

Gordon works so hard to recover. Before his stroke, he spent a lot of his waking hours in his office. He loved his office. It was his own private space where he could think, work, read, and talk on the phone. When he first came home from the hospital, he didn't even look in his office. It is located off the hallway between the kitchen and the stairs to the bedrooms, so he passed by it many times every day. Now and then, he peeked through the glass doors but he didn't walk in or touch anything. Finally, one day he went in and sat in his chair.

For years, Gordon had gone into his office in the morning and made calls and worked on his computer. He was a bit of a tech geek, always wanting the new tech toys, and then rationalizing their purchase by coming up with ways to use them for work. I missed those work noises since the stroke. When he sat at his desk this time, I somehow thought those noises would soon follow. Nope. Gordon called me into his office and asked if I knew how to use a computer.

His memory of his work and how to use any technology was gone—just beyond his grasp. He even had to relearn how to use a telephone. For Gordon, though, wanting to use all his cool stuff was like an instinct. I showed him how to make a call from his cell phone and how to turn on his computer. From that point on, my job was to stay out of his way.

Because his right arm was paralyzed, he took hold of the mouse with his left hand and started moving it around. His typing was limited to just using his left index finger. It was slow, but he didn't care. When he managed to type a sentence it was just a jumble of words that made no sense. Gordon clicked and dragged and experimented and made mistakes and discovered new things every day until he was once again proficient at the computer. It took a year.

Gordon wanted to get back to work. He may have been completely unclear about all parts of his life due to the stroke, but he was perfectly clear about his desire to get back in the saddle as a sales consultant. It just didn't occur to him that he had certain deficits that were going to get in the way.

When Gordon first realized he had a serious language problem, he was shocked. He was so anxious to get back to work that he started making phone calls much too early in his recovery. He taped a phone conversation with what he thought was a potential customer. Before he listened to the tape, he called to me in the kitchen and asked me how he sounded. Hmmmm...loaded question. I said, "Listen to it and you tell me." So he did. It was another terrible moment. I half-expected him to optimistically say, "Hey! I sound pretty good!" Instead, he said nothing.

He was beginning to comprehend the damage done to the language area of his brain. He heard himself saying real words, but they made no logical sense. How could he have clear thoughts in his head but have garbled words come out of his mouth? He was a consultant—how could he ever work if he couldn't talk?

Like many people, Gordon considered driving a car to be an important element of recovery and independence. The only problem with that was he was too damaged to drive safely.

While still in the throes of his stubborn stage, he decided it was time to try driving again. At that point, I was in the middle of teaching our daughter to drive, which was scary enough, and now Gordon? I was pretty sure my heart would not hold up under the stress, but he insisted.

Then I remembered that while Gordon was still in the rehab hospital, one of the staff had mentioned brain injury victims were reported to the DMV and we would have to go there to get his license reinstated. Good! The DMV can be the one to tell him he cannot drive. Happily, I took him to the local DMV, pulled a number, sat down, and waited for our turn.

As we approached the DMV lady behind the counter, she was clearly observing that something was not right with Gordon. I, of course, did all the talking and Gordon stood there, leaning on his cane with his right arm in a support sling. I waited for the magic words, telling Gordon that he would have to take a written test and a driving test in order to get his license reinstated.

Shockingly, those words did not come. Instead, the lady only asked for the fee required to renew Gordon's license. No test! No questions about his ability to drive. Nothing! How can this be?

It turned out there had been no notification to the DMV. Gordon's license had expired, so all we had to do was pay a fee to renew it. He was legally allowed to drive again.

In near disbelief, I commented that Gordon had suffered a stroke and that we had been told he would have to get his license reinstated.

The DMV lady said she could see that something was wrong but she was not allowed to say anything. *Seriously?* Out of fear that they might offend someone or be accused of discrimination, the DMV would rather give a license to drive than require proof of competency?

Gordon was thrilled. He got behind the wheel and drove home. I thought I was going to die teaching Rachel to drive, but I was *sure* I was going to die when Gordon drove. His perception of speed and distance were completely out of whack. He didn't hit the brake until it was almost too late. He drove either too fast or too slow. He didn't look around when he changed lanes. He could drive with his left hand only so turning was jerky and dangerous.

That was the end of his driving for a long time. I didn't put my foot down and forbid Gordon from doing very many things, but driving so early in his recovery was definitely one of those things.

Part of our New Normal is being flexible about our changing roles. When Gordon was in the hospital, I had to learn how to handle everything that a household requires. As Gordon became more aware and clear headed, I slowly handed back some of the duties he was responsible for before the stroke.

He wanted to take back the bill paying. *Yay!* To the best of my ability, I retaught him our accounting system. He wanted more decision-making opportunities with what was going on with the kids. This all seems normal and right—the problem was the ebb and flow of Gordon's abilities. I couldn't rely on him on a consistent basis. Each day was different. I had to be flexible and allow him to try and yet subtly check on him to make sure things were being done correctly. Naturally, it was irritating for him to have me looking over his shoulder, quizzing him.

21

Everyday Life

We began establishing new routines to complement the old routines we were able to salvage.

Walking together was a "must do," not only as a staple of our relationship, but also as a staple of therapy. Since Gordon couldn't swing his right arm as he walked, I held his hand and swung it for him. We started out walking around the high school track. Always the goal-setter, Gordon would ask me to time each lap so he could measure his improvement. His first lap around the track took 20 minutes.

Helping him with his arm allowed him to work on his form and endurance. The exercise itself increased blood flow and oxygen to his brain. Gordon was noticeably more alert and aware when we exercised regularly. When the weather was particularly bad and we did not get outside, his ability to think, speak, work on therapy, and even his balance suffered. I dug out a big golf umbrella and outside we went.

We began saying prayers at night together. I am not sure if Gordon ever prayed outside of a church service prior to his stroke. I don't know if he felt the need or the desire to pray. When he was first in the rehab hospital, I told him he needed to pray for God's help through this time. He looked at me with childlike, wide-eyed honesty. "I haven't prayed," he confessed.

I realize now I was asking too much of him at that time. Yet once Gordon came home, it was time to start a new evening routine of praying together. I helped him shower, shave, and dress for bed. I helped him open his fingers so he could lace his left hand fingers with his right in folded hands fashion. I knelt beside him as he lay in bed and I prayed out loud for the both of us.

In all honesty, I don't think I had ever prayed out loud, other than in church. This was new to me too. Prayers are so personal and private—a conversation between little me and the Almighty Creator. To start praying out loud and reveal this conversation to my husband, even though he is the person who knows me the best, made me uncomfortable. But heck, I was doing so many uncomfortable, personal things for him already, what was one more?

Over time, Gordon became able to shower, shave, and dress himself, and he is certainly able to get himself into bed. He can even lace his own fingers together into praying hands. At about the 4½-year post-stroke mark, he told me he could even say his own prayers.

At first, I was relieved to check prayer time off my list of things to do. After all, Gordon went to bed earlier that I did. I was either doing something with our son or I was just getting some relaxing time in before my bedtime when Gordon would say "Come say prayers with me." I would have to stop what I was doing and get upstairs to finish up his day. He now relieved me of this duty.

And I missed it! Prayer time together was a quiet moment to kneel down and be thankful for all God has done for us. It was our time to bring our concerns and hopes regarding our children to Him. We prayed for friends who were struggling, allowing us to think beyond ourselves for a few minutes and be mindful of others who are suffering. We prayed for wisdom, direction, and discernment. We became aligned in our spiritual life. Such a blessing! Praying together is the one stroke routine we will hold onto for a long, long time.

Once Gordon was released from the rehab hospital, we were instructed to make an appointment with his primary care physician, Dr. S. Since Gordon was no longer under any specialist's care, it was important to establish Gordon's new health status with his doctor. Our first follow-up appointment with Dr. S was an eye-opener as to how mysterious stroke recovery still is.

Dr. S repeated the general wisdom that if a survivor hasn't gotten back certain movement within two years, it probably isn't coming back. He recommended that Gordon take antidepressants, citing an article that showed survivors taking antidepressants had better recovery than those who didn't. Dr. S recommended that Gordon continue taking a statin drug to keep his cholesterol at rock-bottom levels. (Gordon never had high cholesterol, but we cannot allow any build up; instead, we must take very good care of his only functioning carotid artery.) However, he recommended that Gordon take a brand name statin rather than the generic statin that already was working just fine.

Two years. Puzzling. Is there something magical about two years? We also had heard three years was the outside indicator of any recovery. Which was it? Was it either? I asked Dr. S if the two-year mark represented the time when physiologically, the body could no longer get better or if that was actually the time when survivors gave up working on recovery. He didn't know. I asked if antidepressants actually helped with brain function and, therefore, recovery, or if perhaps the medication just helped depressed survivors feel well enough to work on recovery. Again, he didn't know. I asked if the name brand statin would produce superior results in Gordon's health and would be worth the significantly increased cost? He said it was just the statin he most prescribed.

I have nothing against Dr. S. He is a good man trying to do the best for his patients and he has been a pleasure to work with over the years. Yet I had to be Gordon's advocate in every area of his health. That first appointment reinforced for me the need to be informed and to ask questions!

- What will _____ do?

- How will _____ help him?

- What are the risks?

- What should we expect to see as a result?

- How strong is the evidence?

- How new is the approach?

Gordon said that he was not depressed so we did not take up the offer of antidepressants. We kept the generic statin because Gordon responds well to the medication and there was no good reason to change. About six months post-stroke, once Gordon's functioning right carotid artery had healed completely, he was put on aspirin in place of Coumadin, a blood thinner. Gordon's recovery continues long past the two or three year mark. If we keep working on it, we think we will see improvement for the rest of our lives. Every stroke is different.

Because Gordon was a healthy guy, there was really very little that the medical community could do for him. He had no known risk factors. He didn't have an underlying disease that needed to be cured. Other than trips to therapy appointments and annual physicals, Gordon doesn't see a medical professional. Aspirin, generic statin, hard work, and faith equal our prescription for recovery. The responsibility is ours.

22

Back to Work

From the time he was laying in his hospital bed, thinking it was 1985 and guessing Bill Clinton was president, Gordon wanted to get back to work.

Of course, he didn't remember what he did for work, who his clients were, or anything about his professional life, but that didn't matter to him. Whatever he had been doing before his stroke, he wanted to be doing it again—and soon. His drive and work ethic were fully intact while pretty much every other part of his brain was not. Those qualities have been essential to his recovery and without them we would be in a very different place. They are also the qualities that have nearly pushed me to my limit.

In true "Gordon" fashion, he set goals and time frames for himself. When he came home from the rehab hospital, he gave himself six weeks to be out of the wheelchair for good. As soon as the wheelchair was gone, he talked about getting rid of the cane (that took a little longer). And, of course, he wanted to get back to work way too early.

Only five months after his stroke, Gordon started trying to make business calls. To all the businessmen out there who were kind enough to take Gordon's call, try to have a conversation with him, and say something nice at the end—thank you. I am sure you spent a few seconds after the call, looking at your phone, wondering what just happened.

Here is where I come in. I am not in sales. I have never wanted to be in sales. Even the *idea* of cold calling nauseated me. Yet Gordon wanted to start scheduling appointments and there was no way he could do it alone. He couldn't drive, fatigue was still a significant issue, he didn't really know what he wanted to say, and he couldn't say more than a few words in a row before everything either got jumbled up or stopped coming out of his mouth altogether.

What could I do? I could not bring myself to tell Gordon he could not work. I could not trample his desire to recover and resume his life. I couldn't refuse to help him, especially since we knew the real way to recover is by "doing." The only way for Gordon to get back to work was to just get back to work. So we gave it a shot.

It was *way* too early. Some of his old work acquaintances were nice enough to meet with us. On the way to each appointment, we rehearsed certain things for Gordon to say. I asked "What do you do?" and Gordon would try to articulate what he did. He couldn't do it. In broken sentences, he began describing details that didn't matter to whoever might ask the question. He wanted to go on and on about minutiae, not realizing he wasn't answering the question. I wrote a two-sentence answer for him to read, but he couldn't remember it. Every day he read it to me in the car, but not once could he say it in a meeting.

Even worse, at each meeting Gordon would say a few words, then point to me, expecting me to magically know everything that ought to be said. Then, he expected that person to hire him! It was awful. It was painful. It was humiliating. I knew who Gordon had been before the stroke—confident, competent, smart, quick on his feet. Now we sat in coffee shops having uncomfortable conversations with busy professionals while Gordon sat, slumped in his chair, trying to make sense of what was being said, and trying to say something insightful. It was heartbreaking.

And there I was, visibly filled with stress, having no expertise in the subject matter, trying to help Gordon have a coherent conversation. I looked like his babysitter, his mommy. After each meeting, I helped him back to the car where he immediately fell asleep, exhausted by the effort. I drove us home in silence, weighed down with fear for Gordon's health, his recovery, and our financial situation.

Those were dark, hopeless, humiliating, ominous days. But sweet, optimistic Gordon always believed the next one would be better and kept scheduling meetings.

Months went by until finally, Gordon admitted this approach wasn't working. His need for sleep limited his ability to work outside the house, he desperately needed a script to follow due to his speech challenges, and creative solutions were not possible for him at this juncture. Now what?

Be a recruiter! It was *the solution!* He could still work with sales people, he could work from home, and there are defined scripts and questionnaires to follow when interviewing candidates and clients. Gordon wouldn't have to work so hard to originate conversation, and he could rest when he needed to rest. Perfect!

We have a friend who is a successful recruiter and who was willing to train Gordon. We dove in, watching training videos and working with a recruiter to learn the business. Gordon had to sleep every couple hours, but that was okay—we were already at home! We adapted forms to be more one-hand-typing friendly. We made checklists to clarify the process.

We practiced and taped conversations so Gordon could hear himself and identify where his speech needed work. He was making calls to candidates. It all seemed to be going in the right direction! Only one problem—Gordon didn't like it.

After four months, he announced that sales was still his thing and sales consulting was what he wanted to do. My stomach still turns even now, years later, just thinking about it.

Recruiting was such a good plan! Recruiting fit Gordon's needs and abilities! But my will was certainly not being done. It was not about me. You would think I would have known that by then.

23

We Need a Partner

While getting back into sales consulting was Gordon's dream, it was my nightmare. I could not go through the same awful exercise we had done several months before. We could not go about things the same way. It was going to be different this time. This time, we had a partner.

Scott Olsen and Gordon had worked together on many consulting projects prior to Gordon's stroke. Scott was a sales trainer, teaching tactical and strategic selling classes. Gordon was the "hands on" guy, working with the team on process, skills, and staffing. Together, they transformed disjointed sales departments into knowledgeable, effective, and efficient sales teams. Scott and Gordon got along well and respected one another's skills and styles.

Now two years post-stroke, Gordon had slowly regained some of his sales knowledge and had never lost his personal discipline. Scott had excellent communication skills but needed some of that personal discipline to keep his work flow consistent. Together we formed the Olsen Group, with Scott training sales teams and Gordon and me helping implement what they learned.

Gordon was in charge of time management. He established cold calling time, proposal writing time, and brainstorming time. Scott did all the prospective client-faced talking and the computer work. I came along for all meetings and helped Gordon wherever he needed help.

Sounds good, doesn't it? Gordon was so happy to be working in his beloved profession again. He told me over and over how happy he was. The only problem was that Gordon couldn't do the work he wanted to do. He couldn't express himself in order to still be that "hands on" guy. He struggled to communicate with sales people and give them direction and feedback. His brain would lock onto certain words and he would say them over and over rather than explain himself clearly. He became frustrated and would turn to me to speak for him.

The good thing is that I was picking up the business pretty well. I was certainly no expert, but I was learning. But clients were hiring Gordon for his expertise and experience, not for his wife's.

We were settling into an illusion. Scott was speaking for the Olsen Group to land clients and conduct trainings. I was speaking for Gordon in our sessions with sales teams. It looked like Gordon was back to work—but was he?

While the arrangement was productive and we were busy, Gordon wasn't really back to work. We were like a three-legged table. If Scott decided to move on without us, our table crashed to the ground. If I wasn't there to help Gordon, our table crashed again. For Gordon to truly be a sales consultant again, he had to have the ability to be a pedestal table—one central support, only.

Our disability benefits just covered our bills. Those benefits would go away if Gordon was able to get back to work. And that was okay—IF Gordon was able to get back to work. Instead, we were creating the illusion that Gordon was back to work when, in reality, he wasn't. He was able to do a few things related to his profession, but those things were not revenue producing. Because of our arrangement with Scott, we were revenue producing at the moment. We were putting our benefits at risk for something that was not stable or sustainable. Possible scenarios rolled around in my mind.

- Gordon's abilities suddenly flourish and he is able to resume his career. Seriously, why do I even torture myself with that idea?

- For the next 10 years, Scott sticks by our side, the consulting team thrives, and all is well. I can dream, but what are the odds of that happening?

- We earn just enough to lose our benefits, then the consulting team falls apart. Just the consulting team of Gordon and Jill? We have already been down that ugly path.

- We lose our benefits; I go out and find a job. I have been out of the workforce for 12 years. It will take a long time, if ever, for me to earn enough to pay our bills. Gordon would have to be alone every day. With no help, his ability to recover and improve is significantly hindered. Depressing just to think about.

God first. Faith first. Pray. It is all I have left. All the fight and ego in me has been beaten out. No more crying in the closet. No more thinking through possible scenarios, and no more Plan A or Plan B. Surrender.

Our Father, Your will be done. Please take care of us. Please show us the path You have prepared for us and help us follow that path gladly. I have no answers and I am afraid.

For two years we tried to get Gordon back to work. He worked so hard and made huge strides in reviving his knowledge. But language—he couldn't get his words to come out of his mouth. When they did come out, the words were not necessarily the words he intended and they usually were not in the order that made sense.

It also became apparent that our consulting team was at a crossroads. More and more, Scott was being hired for training but Gordon's follow-up coaching was not being requested. Together, Scott and Gordon were sticking to the discipline of marketing themselves and they were getting consulting engagements, but the engagements were for Scott's expertise, not Gordon's.

After two years of trying to be a consultant with the Olsen Group, Gordon realized it was time to stop. He wasn't interested in hanging on, taking a portion of the engagement fee when he wasn't contributing to the contract. Thanks to Gordon, Scott was back on track with his personal discipline of marketing himself. It was time to end it.

Together, we called Scott. Ever the gentleman, I am sure he was thinking about the direction things were going but he was not the kind of man to kick us to the curb. Making the break was the right thing to do. His career was thriving again and he was free to pursue it. We parted as friends.

24

Now What?

So now what? In the first year after Gordon's stroke, when we knew pretty much nothing about the challenges ahead of us, we talked about having a party when Gordon was fully recovered. We thought we would invite a bunch of people for cake in the park and talk about the rough year we had and how we were so happy it was all behind us. So ignorant, we thought we would be throwing that party on the one-year anniversary of the stroke. Yet four years later, with no prospects for our future, no plans, no expectations, we decided to have the party.

For some time, Gordon had wanted to talk about this journey we have been on. He wanted to share our story with our friends and family who had read my blog and supported us, prayed for us, and encouraged us. We were going to have the party and Gordon was going to give a speech.

Gordon went into his office and started typing. Without the use of his right arm, he had to type with his left hand only. Slowly, inaccurately, he typed for days. A couple weeks later, he handed me thirteen pages of broken sentences and misspellings. Then again, his message was clear and I knew what he wanted to say. I just had to help him say it.

Weeks turned into months as I worked on writing his speech. In true Gordon fashion, each day he told me I wasn't working hard enough and that I needed to focus. Please keep in mind that I was not relieved of my other duties—wife, caregiver, mother, cook, housekeeper, gardener, errand runner, etc. Writing is hard enough without all the interruptions and obligations. I occasionally reminded him that I was doing the best I could and that he was welcome to take it back if my work was insufficient. He backed off awhile but after a few days, he was back, nudging me to work harder.

I wrote our story, but that was all it was—our story. It needed something more but I didn't know what.

At the perfect time in the writing process, we were blessed to make the acquaintance of a man named Tom M. Tom had recently sold his company and was taking a break before diving into another obligation. He is highly skilled at giving presentations and took a particular interest in us. Tom had worked for decades to overcome a prominent speech impediment of his own. As he watched Gordon struggle to carry on a conversation, his compassion and empathy were evident. He offered to help us.

I had not realized how personal our story and my writing was to me. I found it difficult to let Tom read the speech. I felt so exposed, so vulnerable. Would he appreciate what we had been through? Would he think I was a lousy writer? It wasn't like I claimed to be a great writer or anything, but I had worked on it for so long, I didn't want someone to tear all that work apart.

In contrast, Gordon couldn't wait to hand it over to Tom and get feedback, criticism, and suggestions. We met a couple afternoons a week at a coffee shop, talking about ideas, flow, and content. Slowly, the presentation came together. Rachel suggested the title, "My Brain Has A Hole In It," which we thought perfectly reflected our humor and our situation.

How was Gordon going to give this speech, however, when the biggest obstacle left from the stroke was his inability to speak? His language was broken and he wanted to talk about it, but those two things don't really go together.

And so, Gordon began to practice. Every evening, Gordon went into his office and read the speech aloud. In the beginning, he had to be seated and he could read only five minutes at a time. He used a small tape recorder so he could listen and critique himself. Slowly he added minutes to his speaking time until he could get through the whole thing.

Then he stood up and tried speaking. The standing part was tiring, so he dropped back to five minute increments. Slowly he added minutes to his speaking time until he could get through the whole thing standing up. Each time, he recorded himself so he could hear how he sounded.

Gordon worked on enunciation—he tended to slur words if he wasn't careful. He also worked on his rate of speech—sometimes he spoke too fast, sometimes too slow. He worked on voice inflection. He was working so hard on saying the words that he tended to speak in a flat tone. His brain couldn't retain the information in the presentation so Gordon had to read every word every time. Every one of his presentation skills needed to be practiced.

He practiced every day for eight months.

On the day of the party, I was nervous, but Gordon was excited. He wanted to look good for the event so he put on a suit and I tied his tie. We rented our church for the evening so everyone would have a comfortable chair. Always looking to improve, Gordon printed a stack of feedback sheets with specific questions and put them on the chairs, along with cheap pens he purchased for the occasion. We were ready.

Nearly 80 people showed up for Gordon's presentation. I stood in the Narthex and greeted each person as they arrived. When everyone was seated, Gordon asked me to say a few words before he began. I thanked everyone for coming. I recounted our ignorance when we thought Gordon would be fully recovered in one year. I thanked everyone for being a part of our recovery and for caring about us.

Then, it was Gordon's turn. Surrounded by the warmth of friendship, Gordon spoke. With only a few stumbles, he got through the whole presentation, reading every word because he couldn't remember any of it, even after eight months of practicing. We laughed, we cried, and we remembered.

At the end, everyone stood and applauded, visibly moved by the enormity of what had happened to us, by the extraordinary progress Gordon had made so far, and by the love that filled the room at that moment.

And then we celebrated! The room roared with laughter and storytelling. People took pictures and we had cake.

Little did we know what was next.

25

A Speaking-Impaired Speaker

The overwhelming feedback we received at the party was that we needed to tell our story to more people.

Medical professionals who have only brief moments with their patients need to see the whole picture. People who are struggling in their lives need to be inspired. People who are suffering need the hope that our story brings. People who as yet are untouched by illness or adversity need empathy and perspective.

Gordon was bursting with excitement. He could no longer improve people's lives through consulting, that was true. But, he could inspire people through our story. He found his new calling: Inspirational Speaker.

He cleared his desk, preparing for his new career. He designed "My Brain Has A Hole In It" business cards and stationery. He created his first website using bits and pieces of the speech as content. He made speaking engagement goals for himself so he could measure his progress.

We wrote email templates for him to send as a warm-up to a phone call. Because his ability to organize his thoughts and words was still broken, we wrote a list of questions for him to ask when speaking on the phone. We tried to anticipate the questions his prospects might ask and wrote the answers for him to read in response. We readied the phone recorder so he could re-listen to conversations later and type notes into his database.

One by one, Gordon began emailing and calling the people listed on the feedback sheets from the party, looking for speaking opportunities and asking for referrals. At first, I had to help with all the calls. Gordon would say hello and introduce himself, then his language stopped. He would turn to me and wait for me to express his words. Each time I explained the awkward gap in conversation to the person on the phone and asked for their understanding as to why I was completing his sentences.

Over time, Gordon was able to make the telephone calls himself. Even now the calls don't always go smoothly with his language issues but that doesn't stop him. He has a scripted explanation for his broken speech.

Slowly but surely, Gordon booked speaking engagements. We go to all the speaking engagements together. Gordon sets up all the technology and gives his speech. I take the stage after him to field questions from the audience. One day he would like to be able to freely answer questions but for now, that is my job and I am happy to do it.

Our interaction with the audience is always deep and meaningful. For men and women alike there are often tears and laughter mixed with thoughtful reflection. People ask about our children and comment on our faith and our marriage. When the question and answer period is over, a few audience members come to speak to us privately. They share their own raw stories of heartbreak and struggle. They trust us with their dark secrets, safe with us.

26

Commitment, Gratitude, and Why Me?

Our commitment to our marriage, our faith, and our family made all the difference. Gordon would not have recovered as well as he has without me as his partner. I would not be even half the person I am today without Gordon, his optimism, and his dogged determination.

Our commitment allowed us to not just survive adversity but to thrive in its aftermath. Our commitment provides our children with a strong foundation on which they will build their own lives and face their own challenges.

Then comes gratitude. We make decisions for ourselves and our view of life. Do we view each day as a glass half empty or half full? I decide every day that my glass is half full. We are now six years post-stroke. Each day, I still remind myself to be grateful. We are still living in our home. We have food, clothing, heat, water. We pay our bills. Gordon's ability to speak improves very slowly, but it improves! We are still happily married. Our children are growing up to be fine, young adults. We laugh every day. We are healthy.

This is not always easy. I continue to have moments where I mourn the loss of our old life. Those moments now come less and less, but they still come. When I feel that loss in my chest, or when I feel fear regarding our future, my new, trained response is to tell it to Jesus. He promised to take care of me and I believe Him. He reminded us that worry will not add a day to our lives and that the Father knows our needs. I am thankful that he listens with love and compassion. I am grateful.

In the aftermath of this horrific stroke, I am happy to say that neither Gordon nor I wasted our time asking "why me?" Why not me? What would make me feel so special to believe nothing bad could happen to us?

I once tried an experiment growing herbs. I planted two basil plants—one stayed in the house in my kitchen window, the other on the step outside our front door. The plant in the window had perfect growing conditions, with lots of morning and midday sun and consistent temperature. It needed very little water. The plant on the front step received the brutal, hot, afternoon sun and suffered the cold of night and the heat of the day. It needed water every day to survive the conditions.

As both plants grew, their differences became obvious. The plant in the kitchen was so weak and delicate, it could barely hold itself up. The leaves were small, fine, and tasteless. It didn't look like any basil plant I had ever seen. In sharp contrast, the plant on the front step was hearty, strong, and prolific with tasty, deep green leaves. It had the kind of leaves you look for at the grocery store, the kind that fill the kitchen with delicious scent when you chop them up.

We are like the basil plant on the front step. We faced difficult conditions. We needed a lot of support to survive from day to day. Yet I like to think we came out stronger on the other end. I like to think we developed good flavor, in the form of perspective, wisdom, empathy, and gratitude.

27

What Is The Plan?

There are still many questions, but I focus on only one: What is God's plan for us? For me?

He is using us and the stroke for something good. Then again, who or what is that something? The part of me that loves to be in control wants to know The Plan.

Perhaps it was for my benefit. Forcing me to withdraw from what was normal life and lean only on Him has changed me. I have always been a confident, competent person. By taking all that is normal away from me, I had to know myself as the broken, lost person I always had been but didn't always acknowledge.

Perhaps it was for the benefit of people I will never know or meet. Maybe someday, someone will experience something similar to what we have experienced. He or she might hear our story and gain hope and encouragement. Maybe someone will be forced to acknowledge their own vulnerability and will turn their eyes to Heaven for the first time.

Perhaps it was the opportunity for all those people who helped us to see themselves differently. When the news of Gordon's stroke got out, amazing kindness and compassion in our community poured in like I had never witnessed before. As Gordon and I continue our walks in the evenings, people still comment that they see us together and feel hope in their own lives because we still hold hands.

Perhaps it was for all those medical professionals that see stroke and other devastating events every day. As we have told our story in various hospitals and clinics, nurses have thanked us for giving them hope for their patients. Therapists have thanked us for showing them that their efforts to rehabilitate their patients can work far beyond the typical time frames. Doctors have thanked us for reminding them, in a tangible way, why they do what they do.

At 4½ years post-stroke, Gordon and I had the opportunity to meet with the neurosurgeon who had performed Gordon's clot retrieval. He showed us the room where the procedure took place and he showed us all the new technology they now use. We asked about his other patients and their recovery. To our surprise, he said he didn't know. He told us that, in all his thirty-some years of neurosurgery, we were the first to come back. Gordon was the first patient he had ever met post-surgery, when his part was over. When he invited us to see the neurosurgery unit, we knew it was special for us, but we had no idea it also was special for him!

It is not for me to know The Plan. It is for me to trust God and look to Him for meaning in my life. The Bible gives us many words of assurance.

My favorites?

> *"For I know the plans I have for you," declares the Lord, "plans to prosper you and not to harm you, plans to give you hope and a future" (Jeremiah 29:11 NIV).*

...in all things God works together with those who love him to bring about what is good (Romans 8:28 NIV).

Trust in the Lord with all your heart and lean not on your own understanding (Proverbs 3:5 NIV).

28

Looking Forward

If I were clever, I would leave this chapter blank and let the empty white page under the title tell the story.

Looking forward is treacherous. When my little planner's brain wants to start playing out possible scenarios of what is to come, the fear from past experience starts pushing back with equal vigor.

Decisions, such as whether we can or should stay in our house, or whether I should be looking for a job, are practical decisions that will need to be addressed soon. Retirement? That may or may not ever be an option, so I try not to even think about it. Travel? I can't let my mind wander to things that are likely out of reach.

When I look forward, I try to think of a bright blue sky. Anything is possible. The good Lord has been so faithful bringing us this far, so why doubt Him now? Maybe He has incredible adventures in store, or maybe He will move us along quietly until our time on this earth is done. Perhaps there is darkness on our horizon. Come what may, I know we are in the palm of His hand and that He loves us.

I am both weaker and more powerful than I ever knew. In my weakness, I was unable to change or prevent any of the awful things that happened, no matter how hard I tried or how much I wanted to. My power came from Jesus, who carried me when I needed carrying and brought me to this place of peace and acceptance. Nothing is going to steal my joy and thanks for this very moment, this very day.

I often review the Bible's most beloved song, a song of trust in God no matter what.

> *The Lord is my shepherd, I lack nothing.*
> *He makes me lie down in green pastures,*
> *He leads me beside quiet waters,*
> *He refreshes my soul.*
> *He guides me along the right paths*
> *for his name's sake.*
>
> *Even though I walk*
> *through the darkest valley,*
> *I will fear no evil,*
> *for you are with me;*
> *your rod and your staff,*
> *they comfort me.*
>
> *You prepare a table before me*
> *in the presence of my enemies.*
> *You anoint my head with oil;*
> *my cup overflows.*
>
> *Surely your goodness and love will follow me*
> *all the days of my life,*
> *and I will dwell in the house of the Lord forever*
> *(Psalm 23 NIV).*

Appendix 1:

What Recovery Has Looked Like
(Gordon's Recovery Path)

Throughout the stroke and our recovery experiences, I struggled with all the unknowns. Yes, "every stroke is different," but even anecdotal information regarding recovery time frames would have been helpful to me. So, here is a general idea of what Gordon has gotten back and when he got it back.

1 month: Began to regain feeling on his right side. Began to ask questions. His right side was so unresponsive that even his toenails felt loose in his feet when I cut them.

Gordon pulls his first prank: Our friend, Teri, helped me bring Gordon home for a day visit from the rehab hospital. When we walked into his room, he was slumped in his wheelchair with a blank stare and the right side of his mouth drooping. I was just about to panic when Gordon perked up, gave us a big smile and said "Just kidding!"

2 months: Sat down in front of his computer and asked how to turn it on. Talked on the phone. Got slight contracting movement in his right fingers. Was able to slightly flex his right elbow. Sleeping 15 hours a day. Used flashcards to relearn math.

3 months: Asked to learn our accounting system again.

Taste buds started to return as feeling began to come back on the right side of his face. Got rid of the wheelchair and now uses only a cane.

5 months: Tried acupuncture but didn't see any benefit. Gordon begins bathing and dressing himself.

6 months: Switched from blood thinner (Coumadin) to aspirin.

10 months: Got rid of the cane. Tries to have business meetings—*way* too soon.

13 months: Tries to drive—we decide he needs more time before this becomes a regular thing.

17 months: With a floatation device under his body, Gordon could kick his way across the pool using both legs.

20 months: Tries to get back to work but speech still too difficult. With my help swinging his right arm, Gordon can walk two miles.

2 years: Remembers having a dream at night. Developed slight rocking movement in his right thumb.

2 years, 4 months: In qualifying to participate in a research study, Gordon met with a neurologist who complimented him on his recovery so far. His comment was: "I have seen your brain scan. I was expecting someone very disabled." Greatest compliment we ever got.

3 years: Sleeping 11 hours at night and taking a nap at lunchtime. Has recovered most of his memory. Fully capable on the computer. We put money in the offering plate at church.

3 years, 4 months: Began practicing his presentation, "My Brain Has A Hole In It," every day. His ability to speak dramatically improves from 3-4 words in a row to 3-4 short sentences in a row.

4 years: Began to get extension in his right fingers. Sleeping 10-11 hours at night and stopped napping. Gave his first presentation of "My Brain Has A Hole In It" to friends.

4 years, 6 months: Can do five push-ups using both arms! Not "girl" push-ups either—*man* push-ups. His right hand is clenched in a fist when he does it, but it is still exciting.

5 years: Right fingers moving but not in an organized fashion. Working on picking up and putting down a pencil. With time, he can open the car door with his right hand and is working on buttoning his shirt using both hands. It took some time but Gordon tied his own sneakers.

5 years, 6 months: Speech continuing to improve but is sporadic. The pattern I notice is that Gordon is best with conversation—I say a sentence then he says a sentence and back and forth. He struggles when he tries to express a series of thoughts or occurrences with no cues to help him.

6 years: Beginning speech therapy in an effort to break through the barrier of logical order in both thinking and speaking.

Appendix 2:

What You Can Do

(Personal Preparedness)

Is it possible to be prepared for every emergency? I don't think so, but there were things we could have done ahead of our experience that would have helped a great deal.

By organizing the following documents and information during calm moments, you can help your loved ones navigate the unexpected more smoothly, and focus energy on the healing process.

- Will

- Power of Attorney

- Durable Power of Attorney for Health Care and general Power of Attorney for any business decision.

- POLST (Physician Orders for Life-Sustaining Treatment)

- Birth Certificate

- Marriage/Divorce Certificates

- License/Passport/other photo ID

- Social Security numbers

- Passwords!

- Banking, investment and retirement accounts information

- How to access computer, cell phone, home accounting system, email accounts

- Payment information for mortgage, utilities, credit cards, any other debt obligation

- Health insurance, life insurance, disability insurance information

- Important contacts, such as accountant, doctor, lawyer, banker, and investment advisor

- Hospital preference

- Medication list with prescription numbers and pharmacy

Decide now with whom to share this information. Make sure they know where to find the information when needed.

If you keep relevant documents in a safe deposit box, does your family member or loved one know where the key is? And, are they included on the signature card at the bank?

Appendix 3:

"If There Is Anything I Can Do..."

We have all said it. Perhaps we really do want to help, or perhaps we are hoping the person will say no! In the midst of catastrophe, hearing those words is difficult. The answer one may want to give is "You can do everything!" but what one typically says is "There is nothing."

How do you articulate your needs when you are in crisis mode? What if you actually make a request and the offering person begins telling all the reasons why he or she cannot do that? Now you are not only in crisis mode, but you are also frustrated and angry with a friend.

I am as guilty as anyone. I have said "Please let me know if you need anything" and done nothing. Not for lack of desire, but for lack of any idea of what to do.

When our crisis came along, we were so blessed to be surrounded by people who did know what to do. Our support system jumped into action, which allowed me to focus on Gordon, the kids, and the things that needed my immediate attention.

So what can you do? How do you be at least somewhat prepared for personal emergency, and what can you do when others are in the thick of it?

The mundane, everyday obligations get put on the back burner when a crisis arises. However, those obligations don't just disappear, and the longer they don't get done, the more stress they cause at home.

Rather than asking if there is anything you can do, suggest specific ways you can ease their burden.

Here are a few practical ways to truly help:

- Set up a communication device for friends and family to keep up with what is going on. Coming home from the hospital every day and having to retell the day's events 20 times on the phone is exhausting. Consider *caringbridge.org* or another communication site where the caregiver can type a message and friends and family can send messages back.

- Are there children at home? Offer to talk to the principal at their school to alert them to the crisis. If the child is going to miss some days of school, establish a method of communication for homework, etc. Are your kids on teams together? Offer to take them to practices and games. Crises are hard on kids—maybe offer a play date to give kids a break from the stress at home.

- Is this a long-term crisis? Disability insurance often takes months to commence payments, while medical bills come almost immediately. Consider setting up a bank account and spread the word that donations are welcome.

- Establish a yard work schedule. If the grass is growing, it still needs mowing. If you and/or a group of people are able to provide this service, let the caregiver know that you will handle the yard for a specific number of weeks/months. In our case, our neighbor paid his gardener to also care for our yard for six months!

- Establish a housecleaning schedule. Even if you can volunteer to vacuum or clean the bathrooms on certain days, that is a huge help. For us, a group of families got together and paid for a housekeeper to come to our house several times. Fantastic!

- Offer to run errands if needed. Be specific! "I can run your errands on _____ days. Let me know what you need."

- Establish a meal schedule. Popping over randomly with this or that to eat is disruptive and generally wasteful. At one point, I had almost three dozen brownies in my refrigerator but no milk or bread.

Be the point person in establishing a meal schedule so the caregiver can plan for food. Are meals what he/she needs? Create a meal delivery plan with delivery times. We kept a cooler by our door and people put the food in the cooler between 5-6pm. No one knocked on the door unless I left a note on the cooler asking them to knock on the door so we could talk.

Do donors want the containers back? If so, they should put their names on them. Are groceries or toiletries what he/she needs instead? Establish a list and a delivery plan.

- Do you have some "handyman" skills? Depending on the nature of the crisis, there may need to be some alterations at the house, such as installing grab bars, moving furniture, etc. If this is a long-term crisis, your skills may be greatly appreciated with general maintenance as time goes on.

- Do you have some items that might be helpful that you aren't using? My friend lent me an extra wheelchair left over from a knee surgery. I was able to have a wheelchair upstairs and one downstairs so I didn't have to haul one of those heavy things up and down. I have been able to lend our shower chair and suction cup grab bar several times since Gordon became more stable.

A few more helpful points to ponder:

- As with anything, to be truly helpful during a crisis, you should do what you say you are going to do—with no surprises. Random acts of kindness are lovely, but in the middle of a life-changing event, help that is reliable and practical is essential. Knowing the day-to-day details are covered allows the caregiver to focus on the major issues at hand.

- Try to keep in mind that this is about helping people get through a difficult time, not about receiving a formal thank you note or getting upset because you don't think your efforts were appreciated enough. Right now, it isn't about you. The person you are helping fully appreciates you and your generosity— they are just overwhelmed at the moment. Be assured, you are doing a good thing.

Acknowledgments

My admiration and thanks first go to Gordon and his relentless persistence, both in his pursuit of recovery and in his belief in me and my ability to write this book. I am lucky to have him.

My admiration and thanks also go to our beautiful children, Rachel and Tom, for weathering the stroke storm with us. They are my pride and joy.

My love goes to my parents, my brothers, and their families. We have never been the most demonstrative or overtly emotional family, but that doesn't matter. I never doubted their love and concern for us, and I knew they would be there to catch me if I needed catching. I couldn't ask for a better family.

A huge smile and big hugs to Gordon's family: his aunts ("the sisters"); his brother Lou, who has the amazing ability to bring joy wherever he goes; and Andrea, for generously sharing her talent for writing by editing drafts of this book several times.

My gratitude goes to the beautiful women in our little Neighborhood Bible Study. One Friday morning every month, they graciously let me cry and pour my heart out over the devastation that stroke brought to our lives. They cried with me, prayed with me, and walked with me through the dark valley of sadness. You have been a gift from God.

To Tom Malone, who entered our lives at the moment we needed him to help craft Gordon's speech, "My Brain Has A Hole In It." You are blessed to be a blessing.

How do I thank an entire community? Care and compassion were evident all over town, from the staff at the kids' schools to the employees at Palisades Market to the nice people who saw us walking through the neighborhoods to our many friends who supported us through difficult times. Thank you Lake Oswego, we love this place.

To the wonderful rehab professionals at the OHSU Center for Health and Healing who have worked with us and our budget to keep Gordon in therapy. Your commitment to Gordon's recovery is a beautiful story of its own.

Thank you to David Sanford and Griff Lindell at Corban University for their enthusiasm and support in writing this book. Every first-time author needs guidance through the writing process, and David was there for me whenever I needed him.

Contact the Viggianos

Thank you for reading Jill's book! She would love to hear from you. You can write to her at <u>Jill@MyBrainllc.com</u>.

You're welcome to share your own story and request prayer by writing to <u>Gordon@MyBrainllc.com</u>.

While you're online, please visit <u>www.MyBrainllc.com</u>, where you can see media coverage of this amazing story, scan a list of places where Gordon and Jill have spoken, read Gordon's often humorous and always true-to-life posts, and invite the Viggianos to speak at one of your upcoming events.

Last but not least, you can call or fax:
- Phone (503) 305-8722
- Mobile (503) 329-8990
- Fax (503) 675-0768

One of Gordon's Blog Posts

Only one more day left.

I can't believe I'm nervous; I haven't been nervous in 6 years. I thought the "nerves gene" was killed off!

Does this mean I'm becoming normal again? Am I supposed to be nervous? Should I postpone the meeting?

All these feeling are turning around inside of me. Why am I stressed? This is the same talk I have delivered more than 100 times. I know it; you think I WOULDN'T feel anxiously.

Maybe this is a GOOD feeling. I hope so! I will let you know how it goes.

Feature Articles

Lake Oswego woman to release book about her husband's recovery from rare stroke
http://www.oregonlive.com/lake-oswego/index.ssf/2014/02/lake_oswego_woman_to_release_b.html

Celebrate World Stroke Day
http://www.mybrainhasaholeinit.com/pages/strokeday.php

Front page and online story in The Oregonian
http://www.oregonlive.com/lake-oswego/index.ssf/2013/01/five_years_after_a_stroke_lake.html

Front page story in the American Heart Association/ American Stroke Association's Portland newsletter
http://www.mybrainhasaholeinit.com/pages/story.php

Oregon Health & Sciences University Brain Institute
http://www.ohsu.edu/xd/health/services/brain/getting-treatment/diagnosis/stroke/gordon-and-jills-story.cfm

Lake Oswego Review, Lake Oswego, Oregon
http://www.mybrainhasaholeinit.com/pdf/The_Comeback_Kid.194221606.pdf and http://portlandtribune.com/lor/48-news/111264-the-comeback-kid

Partial List of Clients

Businesses
- ADP
- Allmed Healthcare Management
- Axium
- ColumbiaSoft
- Entrepreneurs' Organization
- Exterro
- Job Seekers
- KP Financial Services
- Mass Mutual
- Pacific Office Automation
- Phoseon
- Portland Business Partners
- Portland Execs
- Starve Ups
- The Standard
- Vancouver Ford
- Wealth Strategies
- Wellsource
- Winterfest
- Zapproved

Business Professionals
- Crisis Prevention
- Entrepreneurs' Organization
- Kiwanis Club-Portland
- Lions-Boones Ferry
- Lions-Lake Oswego

- Portland Business Luncheons
- Rotary-Camas
- Rotary-Central East Portland
- Rotary-Battle Ground
- Rotary-East Portland
- Rotary-Gladstone
- Rotary-Gresham
- Rotary-Hillsboro
- Rotary-Lake Oswego
- Rotary-Metro Sunset
- Rotary-Milwaukie
- Rotary-Stayton Area
- Rotary-Sherwood Old Town
- Rotary-Vancouver
- Rotary-West Linn

Churches
- Community of Faith
- North Hope Community Center
- Our Savior's Lutheran Church
- Rolling Hills Church
- St. Cecilia Parish Church
- West Hills Unitarian

Education
- Brain Injury Forum
- George Fox University
- Good Samaritan Regional Medical Center
- Guillain-Barre
- Marylhurst University
- North Marion High School
- OHSU
- Pacific University
- Sam Barlow High School

- Tuality Health Education Center
- University of Portland
- Willamette University

Fitness
- American Heart Association
- Club Sport
- Emanuel Hospital
- Good Samaritan Hospital
- Healthcare
- Meridian Park
- OHSU

Senior Centers
- Beaverton Lodge
- Courtyard at Mt. Tabor
- Hearthstone at Murrayhill
- Marys Woods
- Oakridge Park
- Raleigh Hills

Made in the USA
San Bernardino, CA
22 July 2018